The Simple Guide to Starting a Dental Practice and Getting it Right the First Time

By Manfred Purtzki

The Simple Guide to Starting a Dental Practice and Getting it Right the First Time

By Manfred Purtzki, CPA, CA

Blue Beetle Books

First published, 2023
Trade paperback ISBN: 978-1-7778287-4-5

Blue Beetle Books Inc., Victoria, B.C.
www.bluebeetlebooks.com
Tel: 250.704.6686

Inquiries regarding requests to reprint all or part of *The Simple Guide to Starting a Dental Practice and Getting it Right the First Time* should be addressed to Manfred Purtzki at:

Purtzki Transitions Inc.
1700-570 Granville Street
Vancouver, BC
V6C 3P1
Tel: 778-288-2920
Email: manfred@purtzki.com

It is recommended that legal, accounting, and other professional advice is sought before acting on any information contained in this book as each individual's financial circumstances are unique.

The authors, publishers and all others directly or indirectly involved with this book assume no responsibility or liability, direct or indirect, to any party for any loss or damage by errors or omission, regardless of cause, as a consequence of using this book, nor accept any contractual, or other form of liability for such use. The personal services of dedicated professional financial and legal advisors should be sought.

Written in collaboration with Mike Wicks.
Cover design and book layout by Tom Spetter.
Editor: Kara Anderson
Custom publishing services provided by Blue Beetle Books Inc.
Printed in Canada

Also by Manfred Purtzki

The Simple Guide to Selling Your
Dental Practice for More Money

The Simple Guide to Buying
a Dental Practice and
Getting a Great Deal

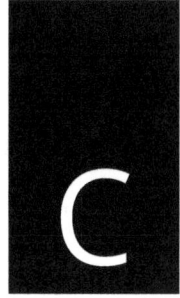

Contents

1

Introduction—Starting Your Practice From Scratch

Let me make an assumption—you have been an associate for a number of years, dreaming of becoming the master of your own destiny by buying an existing dental practice. You have come to this conclusion because you feel your only secure option in today's competitive market is to purchase an existing patient pool that will provide a secure source of income.

However, you are struggling to find a suitable practice to purchase. You have been searching for a long time, and your frustration is building. It has crossed your mind that you could start a practice from scratch—but the risk scares you. You doubt you have the business acumen or entrepreneurial spirit to pull off such an audacious plan. How am I doing so far?

Of course, you may be one of the minority of associates who has the appetite and courage to set out on your own. Whichever category you fall into, I do not doubt that the proposition of starting your own practice scares you to death.

What if I was to tell you that buying an existing practice can potentially carry more risk and requires more business skills and entrepreneurial attitude than a start-up?

I don't blame you if you are shaking your head and thinking "what is this guy talking about?" Please bear with me and allow me to present you with two scenarios. The first follows an associate called Allan, who managed to buy what he thought was a great practice, and the second is the story of Sophie, who started her own practice.

Allan's Story

Allan is a patient man; he spent many years searching for a good purchase opportunity. He considered himself lucky to find what he thought was an excellent practice. Of course, in today's market, he wasn't the only interested party; three other dentists were vying for the three-operatory family practice. His winning bid was $50,000 over the practice valuation of $750,000, which in this case reflected the clinic's annual gross collections. Before taxes and after debt servicing and owner compensation, the net operating income was $300,000.

Allan was delighted with his purchase, but it wasn't long before the bloom was off the rose. He imagined that owning an existing clinic was like driving a bus full of patients and employees. Once he bought the clinic he would take over from the previous driver, and all the passengers would be happy, and the bus would travel along much as before.

However, he quickly realized that the road to Shangri-La—to prosperity and wealth—was bumpy with large potholes. The first jolt hit hard when he discovered that the patient pool was shrinking by around twenty patients per month. Based on the clinic's approximately 2,000 registered patients, that amounted to over ten percent per year. Such an attrition rate was both alarming and unsustainable. This would not have been a significant problem if the clinic was attracting new patients in large numbers, but records showed only six to eight new patients monthly. He had to reverse the trend—and fast.

Let me provide some relevant background to Allan's situation. His clinic is on the third floor of a downtown professional building. This is quite common for older practices, which, when they opened, didn't need street exposure. Two decades ago, dentists were in high demand and short supply. When the clinic opened twenty-plus years ago and built its patient base, most were younger people. Over the years the number of patients fitting this demographic dwindled. Patients married, grew their families, and moved to other areas on the city's outskirts to purchase single-family dwellings. When Allan took over, the remaining patients consisted primarily of single people and retired condo dwellers—and they were aging. When Allan looked at the demographics, he discovered that 80% of his regular patients were fifty-five-plus with limited discretionary income.

His first thought was to ramp up the clinic's marketing. Given the location and the demographics though, Allan was less than confident it would be enough to help, especially in the short term, and the cost would be exorbitant. He knew he needed to upgrade his website and initiate a direct marketing campaign, but he also needed to do something more immediate. So, facing the threat of declining revenues, he turned his attention to expenses to reduce the clinic's overhead, which was 60% of gross revenues.

Allan considered retaining a practice management consultant to increase efficiency, but he got pushback from his staff and abandoned the idea. He then turned to salaries and quickly discovered that taking that route would be like wandering into quicksand. The clinic's hygienists had built relationships with patients over many years. Because of their value to the practice, they earned 20% above the going rate. It didn't take Allan long to realize that pay cuts would result in him losing good hygienists, not to mention the patients who would follow them to their new clinic. Good staff equals good patient retention. Wisely, Allan shelved any expense reduction plan that would affect employees.

He never imagined that taking over what he thought of as a turnkey operation would have so many challenges. He felt that he had bought an old car that was wearing out and needed too many fixes—and he was no mechanic. Apologies for mixing metaphors, but being the driver of this bus was not as straightforward or as much fun as he thought it would be.

Allan's mind drifted back to his worry-free associate days. He didn't have to manage an office or constantly worry about maintaining a positive cash flow. Maybe those days weren't so bad after all. . . Not so fast, let's look at another option and follow Sophie, who approached her dream of owning a dental practice a little differently.

Sophie's Story

Sophie, like most associates, dreamt of owning her own dental practice. The thought of starting her own clinic instead of buying an existing practice had always excited her, but owing several hundred thousand dollars to a bank was scary.

She dreamt of a beautiful, vibrant, well-appointed clinic with a warm, inviting atmosphere in a great neighborhood. However, in her nightmares she saw an empty shell with no patients. It would be up to her to bring in the patients—all of them. Was she up to the job?

She shared her thoughts with her long-time dental assistant and the receptionist at the clinic where she worked as an associate. They were enthusiastic and encouraging, so much so that they said they'd be happy to join her in the new venture. The thought of starting out with an experienced team with whom she worked well took away one of the more immediate stressors of finding and hiring good employees in a tight labor market.

Sophie approached a dental start-up consultant who projected that a clinic could generate $600,000 in its first year, given a suitable location. He helped her pull together a plan to find an excellent high-profile location with enough space for six operatories.

After reviewing her detailed plans the bank gave her an $800,000 loan for the leasehold improvements and equipment, and $200,000 working capital from which she could draw until she broke even in six months, as predicted in her business plan.

Sophie's number one priority was to get patients through the door. She launched a comprehensive marketing program including a slick social media campaign, which generated an average of fifty new patients per month. A key element of her marketing strategy was to open most evenings and weekends. Initially, she planned to cover these herself, but she would bring in an associate when the time was right using the capacity offered by the clinic's six operatories. By being available to patients most evenings and weekends, Sophie found it easy to grow her practice. In the meantime, she sought professional help to set up efficient business systems to ensure the clinic's overhead was a very healthy forty percent.

Recently, Sophie celebrated the first anniversary of her practice start-up. Her supportive start-up team, especially her dental assistant and receptionist, was crucial to her success. Patients love the atmosphere and ambiance of the new clinic, which was designed to Sophie's specific requirements. She still cannot believe that the clinic generated almost $600,000 in its first year—exactly what her dental start-up consultant projected when he submitted the cash flow projections to the bank for financing.

So, who had the most significant risk, Allan or Sophie? They both borrowed a large sum of money and had financial risks. Let's call that a wash. Strategically, Sophie's most significant threat was that she started her business with zero patients, meaning no revenue. All her initial efforts were focused on marketing the clinic. She heavily promoted the clinic to people within walking distance, and she used social media to get the word out to her circle of influence. And let's not forget that she had a unique selling proposition: she would be open evenings and weekends. For patients who worked during the day this was a big pull, even if they were happy with their existing dentist. And that's it! One considerable, but not insurmountable, risk.

Allan, however, was unaware of all the problems (read risks) until after he signed the contract and took possession. He was almost immediately in crisis mode. Declining new patient flow and higher than average attrition rates equaled cash flow challenges that spiraled out of control. Taking over a practice with these issues, or any problems for that matter, requires an experienced business person who understands the remedial action needed to right the ship.

So, which of these two scenarios is the riskiest? I believe, in most cases, starting from scratch is less risky. Undoubtedly, the risk is far more manageable with fewer out-of-left-field challenges. Let me explain.

> **Purtzki's Law:** Starting a new practice is less risky than purchasing most existing practices. First, a startup has more growth potential. Second, when buying an existing practice, the change in leadership style takes a significant amount of management time.

Buying an existing business requires an associate to possess greater entrepreneurial skills. Significant business decision s are forced on them, for which they are usually ill-prepared. Almost anything can throw up a challenge, from dissatisfied staff, old equipment, tenancy issues, and, as we saw in Allan's case, alarming patient attrition.

Starting from scratch allows you time to build your business skills as the practice grows. You will also enjoy being supported by staff members you selected rather than inherited.

Why Start From Scratch?

1. Designing and building your clinic allows you to shape your work environment. You choose the number of operatories, the dental chairs, equipment, lighting, art, the reception area, and the ambiance and atmosphere.

2. You have the freedom to choose a location in a community that offers a growing patient base.

3. You control your time, the patient experience, the corporate culture, and every other aspect of your practice. And, you do it from day one instead of trying to change an environment you inherited.

4. You can build your own team and not have to reshape another dentist's team.

5. You have an opportunity to build wealth more quickly. Given good revenue growth, as in Sophie's example, the goodwill portion of your practice may be as much as $500,000 in the first year.

6. Start-ups usually have better control over operating costs, which are closer to 40% of gross revenues rather than 60%. Higher net income means you have an opportunity for higher take-home pay or cash to reinvest in your business.

The last point above may require a little explanation. Why the 50% disparity in cash flow? Start-up dentists operate on a tight budget by necessity. They make many purchasing decisions and look for the best deals. They also have the luxury of not inheriting the poor deals of a previous practice owner or manager.

In my experience, a start-up's dental supply costs are usually 5% of gross revenues, compared to 10% for established practices. The reason? In existing practices, staff members routinely do the purchasing, and they have little incentive to shop for the lowest price. Also, they often purchase more supplies than necessary to avoid being reprimanded should a dentist require an item that is not readily available.

Starting From Scratch—Two Potential Missteps

My apologies if I have made it appear that starting your own practice is a no-brainer. Let me rectify the situation by giving you two examples of how you can stunt the growth of your new "baby."

Location

When starting from scratch, waiting for the right location will pay dividends. I had a client some time ago; we'll call him Bob, whose primary criteria was owning the real estate that housed his clinic. He was looking at it from an investment perspective. If he was going to work in the practice for twenty years or more, it made sense to be able to sell the much-appreciated real estate with the practice eventually. Neither did he want the hassle of dealing with a landlord, rent increases, the potential threat of demolition clauses, or anything else that might devalue his practice.

However, when Bob searched for a prime retail location, he discovered that although there were many suitable locations, they were only available for lease. Landlords know they can generate more cash from a prime location by leasing instead of selling the property.

Fixated on owning the real estate that housed his clinic, Bob decided to buy a property on a quiet side street off the main thoroughfare. As construction was nearly wrapping up, he noticed another dentist was setting up a new practice on the main road less than a block from his yet-to-open clinic.

Bob's competitor was bustling with passing traffic while his clinic languished on a side street. It wasn't long before Bob struggled to find enough patients to pay his overhead. When he could no longer service his practice debts he was lucky to sell to a dental specialist, albeit for less than he originally paid. It took him several years to recover financially.

Being visible on a busy road is imperative. Other considerations, such as buying the real estate, are secondary.

The Absent Owner

The absentee owner is the second major misstep I often see with new start-ups. Julie decided to make the leap and start her own practice, but she got caught between two worlds. She opened her clinic and saw only a trickle of new patients enter the door. Disheartened, Julie decided to keep the clinic open, manned by a receptionist, but would only work two days a week until it became busier. In the meantime, she worked four days a week in her associate job to pay the clinic's expenses. This may have sounded like a good, safe plan, but the receptionist was turning away new patients every day due to limited appointment availability.

It became a downward spiral; not being able to increase the number of new patients at her clinic meant she relied on her associate job even more. She was trying to do the impossible—be in two places simultaneously. She starved the clinic of its owner's oxygen, and it struggled. Luckily, Julie recognized what was happening and changed her strategy. She began working at her new clinic four days a week, and her appointment book was soon full.

The Four Building Blocks of a Successful Start-Up

Associates regularly ask me how they can successfully launch a new dental practice. The four points below provide the foundation for success. In later chapters, we will investigate them in greater detail, but here are the "CliffsNotes" version for now.

Consult an Expert in Dental Practice Start-Ups

A dental transitions specialist will coach you in setting up and operating a successful practice. You will find it invaluable to have someone by your side who has been through the process multiple times. Beware, there are numerous pitfalls awaiting the unexpected newbie entrepreneur.

Find the Perfect Location

It is best to locate your practice in the community where you live. However, if you have signed a restrictive covenant limiting where you can practice, be careful you are not breaking your associate contract.

The old real estate aphorism, location, location, location, applies to clinics tenfold. Your new clinic should be front and center in a high-traffic street. Avoid side streets and professional buildings, even if you are offered a fantastic deal on the property. As I mentioned earlier, location is more important than the ability to purchase the property. Trust me.

Check out the demographics of any location you are considering. Focus on whether the area is, or soon will be, experiencing growth. New subdivisions and new condo buildings under construction indicate that the area's population is growing. New people moving close to your clinic, potentially without a local dentist, means a steady flow of new patients.

Find a place that has sufficient space. Ideally, look for around 1,800 sq. ft. that will allow for six operatories.

Negotiate a Favorable Lease

Never be tempted to sign a lease that does not contain the following:

- A lease term, plus renewal periods, totaling at least twenty years.

- A no-demolition or relocation clause.

- An agreement that no other clinic will be allowed to open in the building.

- The lease can be assigned to another dentist in the future, with a release from the landlord from your personal guarantees.

- A generous "tenant inducement," i.e., a cash contribution by the landlord to help finance leasehold improvements.

Prepare a Business Plan

Congratulations, starting a dental practice from scratch means you are now an entrepreneur. You now need to start thinking and acting like a business person, and the first call to action is to prepare a business plan to present to the bank. I have seen associates dismiss this as a necessary evil—something they must do to appease the bank. However, if you fail to take writing a business plan seriously, you are making a big mistake.

Embrace preparing a business plan as an opportunity to create a blueprint for a successful business. After all, you wouldn't build a house without architectural drawings or a foundation. You will be investing a great deal of money, so getting it right the first time is crucial.

Someone once told me that it's not just the final business plan document that is most important; it's all that you learn along the way. So true, a business plan helps you answer all the "what ifs."

Your business plan will contain key financial indicators such as your budget for leasehold improvements, capital expenditures, and lease information. Still, several other things can give your business plan the edge when presented to a bank manager, including statements like those listed below.

1. *Patient focus.* Our office design aims to create a comfortable and soothing environment for our patients. We will search for committed staff members who have an extraordinary ability to communicate with patients.

2. *Convenient hours.* The clinic will open non-traditional hours, including workdays to 7 p.m. and on weekends, to gain a competitive advantage.

3. *Strategic location.* The new clinic is located on a busy street with daily commuters. There is also significant pedestrian traffic.

4. *Professional management.* We have retained a practice management team with experience setting up a state-of-the-art business system.

5. *Strong marketing.* We will utilize consultants to implement a marketing program and create a strong brand image for the clinic.

6. *Part-time associateship.* To support the clinic financially during the initial start-up, the dentist will work part-time (i.e., a maximum of three days a week for no more than six months) as an associate generating $10,000 per month.

Make Sound Hiring Decisions

You can have the perfect location, state-of-the-art equipment, and a sound business plan, but it will all be for naught if you fail to hire qualified employees with excellent attitudes. Your first human resources decision should be to hire a first-rate office manager. This person will be the anchor for your clinic and possess a wide range of talents. They need to be confident in setting up all your systems and procedures, and have the experience and personality to work the front desk. Ideally, they will also be a dental assistant, allowing them—when needed— to step in as your part-time assistant.

Some dentists encourage their existing team (from their associate position) to join them in their new clinic. If you consider this, check that your associate contract does not contain a clause prohibiting this maneuver. If it does, there are often staff at nearby clinics who feel underappreciated or underutilized and bored. They will be eager to join a new, exciting practice headed by a young, ambitious dentist. And a considerable benefit of attracting hygienists from nearby clinics is that patients often follow them to your practice.

Currently, the industry—like most others—faces acute staff shortages across the country, so be prepared to pay good salaries and provide attractive working conditions.

Develop Your Leadership Abilities

One reason there are often experienced and desirable employees willing to move practices is that many clinics still employ a command and control management style. These clinics have high staff turnover and will be a good source of experienced staff.

Today, young, progressive dentists engage in a coaching style of leadership. These leaders build teams. They are less authoritarian, ask more questions, offer mentorship, appreciate their employees, and help them develop greater insight into their jobs and performance—all of which spurs personal growth and increases performance. Furthermore, it boosts clinic morale and creates a culture of positivity based on mutual trust and support. Create the right corporate culture, and you will never have to worry about having your staff stolen by a new kid on the block or your associate taking their assistant with them when they leave to set up their own clinic.

Leadership is crucial to your long-term survival. I recommend you invest in your future by hiring a leadership coach.

I hope this opening chapter has excited you about the possibility of starting your own practice. Chapter Two discusses what makes for a perfect location in more detail.

2

Location, Location, Location

In Chapter One I outlined the pros and cons of starting your own dental practice. In the past, most associates bought an existing dental practice; today, a new breed of dentist is making itself known. These young dentists have no intention, or desire, to buy an existing dental practice.

Starting out on your own is not for the faint-hearted. However, if, like a white-water kayaker running the rapids, you feel that successfully negotiating dangerous waters is more exciting than off-putting, let me be your guide. I'll help you navigate the many challenges ahead and maximize your chance of starting a practice that will give you a rewarding career, financial security for you and your family, and a solid retirement strategy.

In this chapter, we take a deep dive into the first building block of a successful start-up: choosing a location that works for both the short term and the long haul.

Emily's Story

Emily has been working as an associate for four years and is one of the new breed of dentists I mentioned earlier. She views her associateship as a way of earning her stripes, developing her technical skills, dealing with patients, and understanding how to manage a clinic, all the while dreaming of how, in her own practice, she would do everything better.

She feels the time has come to move on with her career. Like many of her friends in dentistry, she has no desire to buy an existing practice. She plans to build her practice from the ground up, so finding a suitable location is the first step.

Over coffee, a couple of commercial realtor friends ask her what her vision is of a suitable building and location. What are her criteria? What neighborhood is she considering, and how much space does she need? What type of building? Is she buying or leasing? The questions come thick and fast, and Emily realizes she needs expert help.

Emily made the right decision and brought on board an expert in dental practice start-ups to assist her. Failure is not an option when starting your own dental practice. You will be borrowing a ton of money from the bank, and if the clinic is not a success, how will you ever repay the loan? It's a one-shot deal. I know that's a scary thought, but before you run for the hills or back to your associateship, let's follow Emily—she seems to be heading in the right direction.

After her coffee meeting, she began to appreciate what she didn't know—which was a lot. She called a few of her industry friends and asked if they knew of a dental practice start-up guru. Overwhelmingly, they recommended Michael as the go-to guy. She checked him out and discovered that he was a CPA who, for the past 30 years, had lots of experience in dental start-ups. Perfect!

A few weeks later, she had a Zoom meeting with Michael. She first asked him how he worked with young dentists wanting to start their own practice. He explained that his role was to advise and help her navigate each phase of the practice start-up. He listed finding a location, arranging bank financing, and marketing the clinic as the three main items.

During the meeting, Emily explained that her dream was to purchase a lot and build a clinic to her specific design. Before Michael could jump in, she said she appreciated that the price of commercial land in the city made this impossible, so she planned to move to a rural community. To demonstrate that she has thought this through, she quickly said that she felt a smaller community would offer a much greater chance of successfully growing her practice than the city, where the competition for patients is fierce.

Michael waited for her to finish and agreed that there were benefits to a small community, such as more affordable building lots and less expensive commercial leasing opportunities. And, parking would not be the issue it is in the city.

At this point Emily nodded vigorously, but Michael said, "However, you should not underestimate the opportunity for growth in a city location, which can usually be greater than that of a smaller community." Emily was confused at what she felt was an about-turn and asked Michael to explain why, with so much competition, growth could be better in the city. Smiling, he said that city dental practices that opened on Saturdays were hectic, and those appointments were popular and booked up quickly. "If you open a clinic in the city and offer weekend appointments and weekday spots as late as 9 pm, you will attract new patients who can only make those times. Many city clinics don't offer Sunday or late weekday appointments, so these would not be competition to your new state-of-the-art clinic offering flexible appointment times."

Emily countered, "But as soon as I opened my doors and offered all these non-traditional appointment times, wouldn't my competitors just copy me?" Michael explained how difficult it is for a clinic to change its hours once it has established an 8 am to 5 pm routine. The operational changes required are significant and costly. Additional staff need to be hired, there could be issues around the building or mall opening hours, and new schedules need to be developed. Even if the owner and associates were willing to incur the extra cost of hiring staff to accommodate Saturday and Sunday openings, the clinic's regular patients would immediately begin taking the prime weekend spots, resulting in fewer spots for new patients. It would also negate the justification for extended opening hours and increased operational costs.

Michael said that he had witnessed several established city clinics aggressively expand their weekend hours, only to revert to their original Monday to Friday openings because the weekend hours were not financially feasible. Emily jumped on this and asked, "Why would it be financially feasible for me then?" Michael explained that building longer opening hours into the start-up business plan was vastly different from reinventing the wheel later.

Emily looked unconvinced and said she still felt that a rural community offered a better opportunity for a new dentist, especially one that opened on weekends and late on weekdays. Michael warned that patients in rural communities and small towns are very different from those in cities and were less likely to utilize extended opening hours.

To make Emily aware of another risk associated with opening a practice in a smaller community, Michael told her the story of William, a client of his. The latter moved to an idyllic, small lakeside community. William loved the outdoor life. As an avid paddleboarder and angler, living by the lake was perfect. When he opened his practice, he was one of only two dentists in town. His competitor was busy, and appointments to see a hygienist were in short supply. Still, it took time for him to be accepted—for people to become comfortable enough with him to switch dentists—despite his clinic's state-of-the-art equipment, and his flexible schedule.

Eventually, patient numbers began to rise, and it looked like the practice would be successful. Then, one day, he noticed a sign on an empty storefront announcing a new dental practice. At first, he wasn't too concerned; his patients seemed pleased with him and he'd built a solid relationship with them. Everything changed when, through the grapevine, he learned that the new dentist was the daughter of a prominent community member who was president of the Rotary Club. Once the new clinic opened, his patient attrition was out of control. Patients began moving down the street to the hometown dentist in droves. After all, many had known her since she was a child; it would have been rude not to support her. Michael shrugged and told Emily that it's hard to be a newcomer in a small community. Relationships run deep in communities.

After the Zoom call, Emily reflected on the conversation. Everything Michael had said made sense, and his cautionary tale of starting a practice in a small community was a huge reality check for her. Despite the competition, she began to see why the city might be a better option. Grateful to Michael for the reality check, she decided to redirect her energy into looking at a city practice. They agreed to meet in person over lunch the following week.

Michael's point to Emily regarding how patients act differently depending on the type of community they live in is worth exploring further. Before we do that, however, note that most people use a dentist where they live, not where they work.

First, let's look at a coastal town of 30,000 people. Dentists here are open Monday through Friday and are closed Saturday and Sunday, and most don't offer late weekday evenings. The reason is, for the most part, people work locally or have a modest commute and have little difficulty finding suitable appointment times during regular opening hours.

Now, let's visit a commuter-belt community of 60,000, an hour's drive away from a large city center with a population of almost 700,000. In this case, dentists are busiest over the weekends and later in the evenings on weekdays. The reason? Patients work in the city. Most patients can't make weekday appointments until after they return from work. I have many clients in communities like this who have had great success opening from noon to 8 pm during the week. Surprisingly, they experienced little trouble attracting staff to work this shift.

Finally, dentists rarely open on weekends in smaller rural communities or offer late appointments during the week. In this case, patients are busy on Saturdays taking their children to sporting activities, and on Sundays they enjoy nature, going to church, or resting. The pace in a smaller rural community is less frantic, and people make time during the week to fix their teeth.

Emily and Michael meet at a local downtown restaurant. She chose the restaurant because of its central location in an area of town she felt might be a good place for her clinic. She ordered a chicken Caesar, and he went for the Thai Buddha bowl. Waiting for the food to arrive, Michael said, "Let's talk budget, Emily." From a previous conversation, Michael knew that Emily has no financial reserves. On the upside, she recently paid off her student loan. Emily says she will only have whatever the bank will lend her. Michael smiled, "Then first we need to get a preapproved loan, which will be our budget."

Once the food arrived, they began to discuss suitable locations. Emily reeled off several possible sites her realtor friends had sent her, but Michael held up his hand. "The first thing we need to do is list the criteria for a great clinic location. Number one on the list is high visibility; that is crucial." He clarified that second floors were not an option for a start-up; they cost less, but it's a false economy. For instance, a good location would be a ground-floor retail space on the main street with commuter traffic. He told her that a busy sidewalk with pedestrians would generate many new patients. She might consider a busy commercial plaza or shopping mall. The key, he emphasized again, was visibility, which meant a ground floor location was non-negotiable.

Michael questioned how much space she needed. Glad to be on solid ground, she answered confidently that the minimum would be 1,200 sq. ft., allowing enough room for four operatories. However, 1,800 sq. ft. would allow for growth to six operatories, which is what Emily projects the practice will grow to over the next twenty years. This requirement means she needs to find a space that offers long-term occupancy. Moving locations down the line would be prohibitively expensive and could result in significant patient attrition, depending on the distance.

Purtzki's Law: Stretch your budget to get at least 1800 sq. ft. This will allow space for six operatories. The early financial sacrifice will be rewarded many times over by never having to move to another location in your career.

Emily was sold on the fact that Michael was the expert and that she needed to let him do his thing, so she just nodded when he said, "Okay, Emily, I'll pull together a financing package for the bank, the central plank of which will be the cash flow projection. We will need to have all our ducks in a row because once your offer is accepted on the building, we may only have three or four weeks to get the financing approved." Emily promised to get all the baseline figures to Michael as soon as possible, and they agreed to keep in touch via email.

Preparing everything for the bank is vital to ensure loan preapproval goes smoothly. I have seen several instances where a dentist lost a dream space because the bank could not meet the deadline. Emily has a lot to do to prepare the package for the bank. One of the first things is to weigh the difference between leasing space that will accommodate six rather than four operatories. It's not just the leasing costs but the extra construction cost. Investing in the larger space will make sense if she believes she will outgrow a four-operatory clinic in ten years. The ability to increase capacity by fifty percent later is a valuable asset, and she wouldn't need to purchase the additional chairs and equipment until that space is required.

Michael and Emily haven't discussed purchasing a retail unit instead of leasing it, but it is an option. The challenge is that there are far fewer purchase options than leases. Purchasing is, without a doubt, the preferred option because of the long-term appreciation of real estate. It also removes the chance of landlord—tenant conflict over lease rates, operating expenses, lease renewals, and the dreaded demolition clauses found in many lease agreements. There are two caveats to purchasing a unit or building; first, never compromise the visibility of the location just because you can buy the space, and second, be cautious when purchasing a unit from a developer with other units for lease in the same project. Developers tend to retain the premier units to lease themselves, which may have better street exposure and a better floor plan. Also, get some assurance in writing that they will not rent or sell another unit in the same project for use as a dental clinic.

You should look for lease terms with renewal periods covering thirty to forty years when leasing. The advantage to you is that you can sell the practice when you decide to retire, and the incoming dentist's tenancy is assured for fifteen or more years. For this reason, look for a newer building that is unlikely to be demolished during this period.

A few months later, Michael emailed Emily to say that the bank had pre-approved financing for an 1,800 sq. ft. lease space. Purchasing space was a non-starter for Emily as she didn't have a down payment. He suggested they meet the next day as he had come across a listing on a suitable corner unit in a newly completed commercial development.

Emily was immediately impressed when they visited the development. The unit fronted two busy streets, and people walked back and forth right past the front door. Michael pointed to the unit next door; it was a high-end hair and esthetics salon. Emily recognized this as an excellent source of patient referrals. It was perfect; she told Michael this was it and asked him to put the wheels in motion to obtain the lease. He said that before she got too excited, he would make a checklist of everything they needed to get information on before making a firm decision and get back to her the following day.

> **Purtzki's Law:** Location is the biggest driver of future growth, so don't compromise. Hold out for a location on a busy street, with lots of vehicle and pedestrian traffic.

Michael was correct to tell Emily not to get blinded by a desire to seal the deal on such a fantastic location. Due diligence may be tedious, but it can save you a ton of money and heartbreak in the long run. You need to check these key things before you consider signing a lease.

Zoning

In Emily's case, the landlord had assured them that the zoning allowed for a dental clinic. Still, Michael knew from experience that confirming it with the local planning department was the first step in due diligence.

Signage

Prominent signage is critical; you need people to know you are there and that you are a dental clinic. It's no good finding a strategic location, like Emily, with exposure to two streets if you are not allowed to have stand-out signage, especially as a start-up. Many landlords have strict rules governing what signage you can and can't have. Checking this out before you sign on the dotted line will save you from protracted negotiations at a later date. It's not only the landlord that has a say in what signage you can have; you will need to check out local signage bylaws with City Hall. Of course, a first step should be figuring out your budget for signage. There is no point fighting for signage you can't afford.

Parking

You rarely get the parking you want or need, especially in the city. You will be lucky to get a few designated parking spaces for your staff. In Emily's situation, Michael asked her to think of herself as a patient and try to park at different times of the day and week. How easy was it to park? Were there meters nearby, a parking garage, or free side street parking? If Emily found the location congested and experienced difficulty finding a parking spot, should she reconsider the location? Possibly. But, with a bit of creative thinking, it could be a competitive advantage. Imagine finding a perfect location. You love it, but the parking situation is awful. Consider that other people may not have jumped on the unit for this very reason. You have two options, pass on leasing it or find a way around the parking issue. Creative thinking might solve the problem; why not hire a parking valet, as you see outside fancy hotels and restaurants? This may not, at first, seem a budget-friendly option, but if you consider it part of your marketing budget it could be cost-effective. It would give you a unique selling proposition that would wow patients and even have the capability of attracting patients from other local dentists. If you let the local media know you were offering a valet service, they would almost certainly make it a news story. Start-ups need to be creative.

Usable Space

Answer me this: when is 1,800 sq. ft. not 1,800 sq. ft.? The answer is when it includes a portion of common areas not devoted to your specific use (e.g., a percentage of the lobby and hallways). Ensure the space quoted by the landlord is all available for your clinic. The unit's layout will determine where you locate your reception area and operatories. 1,800 sq. ft. is usually sufficient to allow for six operatories, but not always. For instance, if you've found the perfect location on the ground floor of a residential building, the space and layout may look perfect, but beware, there may be electrical lines and pipes running through the floor. Why is this important? Because it will limit the floor area you can drill through to install chairs and other equipment. I have seen many dentists have to install fewer operatories than planned because they ran into this problem. Get the mechanical drawings from the landlord and study them before committing to the unit.

Patient Demographic Analysis

Finally, understand the neighborhood's demographics where you plan to locate your clinic. Michael did the following demographic analysis for Emily and discovered some interesting nuggets of information.

1. More than 70% of people in the neighborhood travel downtown for work. Most of these commuters use a dentist close to their home. Therefore, there would be a fantastic opportunity for Emily to attract new patients by being open after hours, including on evenings and weekends. Setting the clinic hours from noon to 9 pm Monday to Friday would make sense to capitalize on getting this commuter business.

2. The local population has a higher than average education. There is a positive correlation between a patient's level of education and their dental IQ, which usually translates into more lavish spending on dental treatments.

3. This city area has more people in higher income brackets than the average population, indicating that patients are likely to be more receptive to high-end treatments.

Michael and Emily met for coffee a few days later and went over the results of the due diligence exercise. After a brief discussion, they agreed that negotiations for the lease contract could now start in earnest.

3

Negotiating the Lease

You've found a great location, the space is exactly what you need, and you are raring to go—but hold on, you are about to enter into dangerous waters—the lease. You get one shot with a lease; once you agree to everything it contains it is set in stone. The commitment is such that you won't be able to change as much as a comma. If that's a scary thought, good. Many pitfalls lie waiting for you on your journey to getting a lease you can live with—that you will have to live with. Sure, you can probably extend the lease later, but the rent amount is the only thing likely to change.

In most cases, the "landlord" will be a corporate entity, not a person; in either case, don't be surprised if negotiations turn confrontational. It often depends on the market as to who has the upper hand. If vacant retail space is abundant and the landlord has been advertising for a long time, the tenant has a bargaining advantage. The reverse is true; if ten people are vying for the space you want, you significantly diminish your bargaining power. In my experience, metropolitan areas have experienced a shortage of good retail space for some years.

In my early career as a dental start-up business consultant, the rental business was a little simpler; you dealt with the company's owner in person—the landlord—read a reasonably simple lease, negotiated the details, signed it, and moved in. Today, the lease you will review will likely be a simplified version. Your lawyer will review the full version of the lease. Hopefully, they have experience dealing with leases for space specifically to be used for a dental clinic and protect you from anything egregious. The big question is, who negotiates with the "landlord?" There is much to consider that is specific to using space for a dental clinic, which I will cover in this chapter, so you may think it should be you handling the negotiation. However, I recommend that dentists never meet, let alone negotiate with, the landlord or their representative. Meeting the landlord is best left to your dental start-up consultant.

Don't let your lawyer negotiate your lease; they are often inflexible and uncompromising. Leave this to your dental start-up consultant; they will get you the best possible deal.

> **Purtzki's Law:** The lease you sign will remain in force for as long as you occupy the premises. You must get it right the first time. There are many lease provisions unique to the dental profession, so it is vital you retain a dental expert.

The difficulty with lease negotiations is that they are a zero-sum game. There is no win-win; a monetary gain for one side is a monetary loss for the other. However, you have an advantage; dentists are one of the most desirable tenants. Why? Because they have financial stability and desire long leases. The challenge is that this advantage becomes less significant in a tight leasing market. The big takeaway is: stay out of the lion's den.

Let me explain why getting expert help working with landlords is money well spent. The primary focus of a landlord is to obtain the highest possible lease rate. Attempting to get a lower rate will be tough. Let's look at why landlords are so obsessed with the rental amount. The rental amount defines the property's value, so if you were to pay an additional $250 per month ($3,000 annually), the landlord will, if we assume a three percent rate of return, see their real estate value increase by $100,000.

However, by focusing on ways the landlord can decrease your financial burden, you can negotiate a far better deal. A dental start-up consultant will arrange a longer free rent period or a larger tenant improvement allowance. One-off payments are more acceptable for landlords than "losing" a percentage of the rent for the duration of the lease.

In short, rather than trying to reduce the rent, use it as a bargaining tool to get what you want right now; for instance, to get a thirty year lease, six months free rent, and a $50 per square foot leasehold improvement allowance. On an 1,800 sq. ft. space, that $50 equates to a $90,000 lump sum—heaven-sent when dealing with an extensive construction budget.

The Offer to Lease

The offer to lease is the document you will review; it will have all the relevant information about your lease agreement. It is not the full, legal lease, which is the document your lawyer will review. The points below detail the main terms and components of a typical lease offer and provide some advice based on my thirty-plus years of experience.

1. **Premises:** The first question you must ask yourself is how does the rentable area compare to the usable space? I know that sounds like I'm playing with fine lines, but as I discussed in Chapter Two, it has become common for landlords to add a percentage of common areas, such as hallways and lobbies, into the unit's square footage. This practice could mean that your 1,800 sq. ft. contains only 1,600 sq. ft. of usable floor space, meaning one less operatory. Another issue to consider is the space layout; if it is an unusual shape, you may have difficulty fitting in everything you need.

2. **Basic rent:** The rent the landlord receives, excluding operating expenses (i.e., before you pay your share of hydro, water, etc.).

3. **Term:** The lease's initial term is usually five or ten years.

4. **Commencement date:** The date when you start paying rent.

5. Fixturing period: The time, usually four to six months, you have available to build out the space before you start paying rent. Of course, landlords will negotiate the shortest period they can. Consult with a builder, or multiple builders, and get a construction timeline. This timeline should include the time it will take to obtain building permits (a three or four month delay is not uncommon). The landlord will likely propose a shorter period, but you should insist on the timeline given by the professionals you have retained. Remember the adage that whatever can go wrong will go wrong, so even a qualified contractor's estimate will likely be optimistic. I have witnessed dentists who paid rent when their clinic was months away from welcoming patients.

6. **Free rent:** Negotiate hard for the best deal you can get on the free rent period. This is another occasion where your dental start-up consultant will earn their fee. Remember, this is in addition to your fixturing period, which means your rent will be covered if construction runs longer than the period you negotiated. One word of caution: during

the free rent period, you are still responsible for paying the operating costs (see below).

7. **Operating costs:** In addition to basic rent, you will be responsible for a proportionate share of operating expenses: property taxes, insurance, repairs, maintenance, etc. The landlord should stipulate the estimated square footage cost for the first year, for instance, $8 per square foot. The landlord must show you the calculations to support the operating costs.

8. **Deposit:** Once your offer is accepted, you will typically provide the landlord with a deposit. The landlord usually holds the amount without interest. I have seen cases where landlords have held this deposit indefinitely. Be sure to add a line to the contract that states the deposit will be applied to your first and last month's payment of the basic rent.

9. **Landlord's work:** This section stipulates improvements the landlord is responsible for to ensure that the space is ready for the specific requirements of a dental clinic. Landlords are responsible for electrical capacity, plumbing, HVAC, demising walls (walls that separate your clinic from other tenants' spaces and common areas), etc.

10. **HVAC:** You, as the tenant, will be responsible for repairs and maintenance to the HVAC system in your clinic. However, ensure that the lease stipulates that the HVAC system's replacement is the landlord's responsibility and that they will absorb the cost. I have witnessed many conflicts over this issue between dentists and landlords.

11. **Tenant improvement allowance:** Payment of this allowance occurs after construction is complete. The landlord will usually require a satisfactory statutory declaration stating that you have settled all accounts for the work, services, and materials and that there are no liens against the premises.

12. **Improvement allowance on lease renewal:** Remember, you plan to remain in the space for maybe twenty years and beyond. Think ahead and add into the lease agreement that, at the ten-year point, you will expect the landlord to grant an additional improvement allowance so that you can upgrade and modernize the premises; this is a reasonable expectation. The landlord has enjoyed a steady income for the previous decade, and any improvements increase the property's value.

13. **Options to renew:** Negotiate as many lease renewal options as possible to ensure your tenancy for a minimum of twenty years. Multiple renewal options are crucial if you expect to be able to sell your practice when you decide to retire. The value of your practice at that time will be proportionate to the number of years of undisturbed tenancy the buyer will enjoy.

14. **Use of premises:** This is simple; you need to state that your purpose is to provide dental services.

15. **Exclusivity:** There must be a clause stating that the landlord will not lease space to any tenant that will compete with your business.

16. **Parking:** Never underestimate the importance of parking availability. From the outset, negotiate as many spaces as possible. Ideally, you are looking for dedicated parking for you and your staff. Parking is tricky; landlords often have an overarching policy relating to parking allocation. As discussed in Chapter Two, consider parking availability at the location before committing to a lease. If parking is limited, it can affect your growth.

17. **Signage:** You will be required to provide the landlord with drawings and specifications for their approval of all the signage you plan to use. The lease offer should stipulate that all signage will be subject to the city bylaw and municipal approvals. As mentioned in Chapter Two, negotiate as much signage as possible. Nothing beats a good-looking sign that drivers and pedestrians can see.

18. **Assignment:** This standard clause states that although the lease assignment is subject to the landlord's approval, it will not be unreasonably withheld. A landlord withholding assignment approval can be hugely problematic down the line when you decide to sell your practice to another dentist. A landlord could state that they are reasonably withholding permission because the incoming dentist has little or no worth compared to you, who will be a high-net-worth individual by that time. I call this the doomsday scenario. You started your practice from scratch, it's now worth well over a million dollars, but you can't sell it. I advise adding to the assignment clause that you will not require the landlord's consent if you assign the lease to another dentist. This simple step can save you a great deal of heartbreak two decades into the future.

19. **Indemnity:** Landlords will often ask you and your spouse to guarantee the lease payments personally. Many dentists, quite reasonably, are unwilling to have their spouses sign a personal guarantee. This request is negotiable—and you should know that it is not common practice—so feel free to dispute this requirement.

    More important is that you ensure the lease explicitly states you will be released from your guarantee on the lease assignment. You do not want to be in a position where you guarantee the lease payments of the new owner.

20. **Demolition clause:** Ensure the lease does not have a demolition clause, a redevelopment clause, or a termination on notice clause (the latter could allow the landlord to end your lease for any reason). A demolition clause is lethal. You will never be able to sell the clinic if such a clause exists. Even if you could find a buyer willing to ignore the clause, they would never get financing. Also, beware of the delayed or future demolition clause. Ensure the lease prevents the landlord from adding a demolition clause during lease renewals. Note: When it comes to lease extensions, the lease stipulates what the landlord and tenant can change when executing the lease extension. Normally, this is only the lease rate. For example, the landlord cannot put a demolition clause into the extension, unless the original lease provided for it. The bottom line is, the landlord can't come up with a new lease, on a lease renewal.

21. **Relocation:** Here is another potentially damaging clause; don't accept a clause that allows the landlord to relocate you to a different part of the building. You chose your location because it suited your needs and hopefully had excellent exposure. Relocating involves uncertainty, disruption, loss of earnings, and many additional expenses. Your practice goodwill will inevitably take a hit, depending on the location. Also, a potential buyer would be wary of moving into a clinic where the landlord could invoke a relocation clause.

22. **Death and disability:** Ensure that the lease can be terminated on short notice, without additional costs, in case of your death or long-term disability.

23. **Tenant's conditions:** Tenant conditions might include:

    a. The ability to review and approve the landlord's "offer to lease" and have a lawyer review the complete, legally-binding lease agreement.

b. Approval of construction costs for leasehold improvements.

c. Obtaining adequate financing.

24. **Landlord's conditions:** Landlord conditions might include:

a. Permission to review and approve the tenant's financial information to establish their creditworthiness. Financial credibility is not usually an issue with dentists.

b. Review and approve any changes proposed to the landlord's standard lease form.

Other Considerations

Removal of Conditions

The offer to lease stipulates the date the tenant's and landlord's conditions must be satisfied, or the offer will collapse. Landlords are keen to see conditions removed as soon as possible, usually within a month. A month may seem reasonable, but I have seen multiple offers collapse because the bank loan approval did not come through in time or its conditions were unacceptable. You can ask the landlord for an extension, but you may not get it and could lose the ideal location on which you were banking. Landlords often have other people, including other dentists, waiting to take your place if you falter. I advise that you arrange preliminary financing approval when you start looking at locations, not when you have found a desirable home for your clinic. If you decide to hire a dental practice start-up consultant, they will have long-term relationships with banks, which will help fast-track the process.

Review of Landlord's Lease

Landlords like to talk about a standard form of lease. The word "standard" is used as a ploy to make you think that it is normal, and that all other tenants have agreed with it and signed it—basically to give you a false sense of security. They hope this strategy will result in you asking fewer questions. I've been in this business for thirty years and have never seen this mythological "standard lease;" it doesn't exist. When it comes to a lease, invest in a lawyer specializing in reviewing and preparing dental clinic leases. I guarantee it will be money well spent. Not only do they have the experience to spot all the things I have warned you about in this chapter, but they will negotiate with the landlord so you avoid any confrontation. Let them fight it out; you're a dentist, not a lawyer. Besides, this type of negotiating can be massively time-consuming. As I mentioned earlier, this is a big commitment. Once the lease is signed, the landlord will not revisit it to make changes. It could be in place for thirty years.

Construction Costs

You must handle your construction budget professionally if you expect your landlord to approve the design and blueprints. The first thing I suggest is hiring a contractor and designer specializing in the construction of dental clinics. Dental clinics differ from retail stores or offices; for instance, they need specific connections for water and power. Remember in Chapter Two, we looked at usable space and being able to drill into floors to install an operatory? That is why you need contractors who understand the challenges of building a dental clinic in an empty unit. They will be able to assess the implications of the mechanical drawings and their impact on your specific circumstances and technological challenges.

Once your contractor is satisfied that you can build out the space without restrictions, the designer will prepare a preliminary design for your approval; this will provide the remaining information to allow the construction contractor to prepare a budget.

During the period lease conditions are removed, you will be very busy working on the design with the architect, obtaining competitive quotes from contractors and tradespeople, and making decisions on equipment and cabinetry. Never skip the essential steps when checking out the space because you are under time pressure. Rather than compromising, ask for an extension of the lease offer.

4

Partnering for Practice Start-Up

The perceived risk is one of the biggest things that prevents young dentists from starting their own practice. They have the dream, but borrowing $800,000 to set up a clinic is not chump change—it's scary. If this describes you, then you have probably worried about whether you could bring enough patients through the door to pay the bills and the loan. I have known people like you who have had restless nights dreaming about the doomsday scenario of defaulting on a bank loan and being deemed a lousy credit risk for the rest of your days. All this is true. There is a risk—all business involves risk—but dentists are one of the most secure credit risks, which is why banks are happy to loan large sums of money to them. It is very rare for a dentist to default on their loan payment. As start-ups go, dental clinics are a safe bet.

Are you feeling less concerned about the risk involved? If not, it may be worth considering finding a compatible partner to halve the risk. However, splitting the financial risk doesn't mean there aren't other risks to consider, as we will see later in this chapter.

Putting the risk aside for a minute, many associates look to partner in a new clinic so they can share the management responsibilities and time commitment. Starting and running a dental practice solo can be as much a time burden as a financial liability. My consulting practice is seeing work-life balance become increasingly important to today's incoming cohort of dentists who want to set out independently.

Another reason you may need to consider partnering with another dentist is that the bank denied your loan request because it exceeded the amount they were prepared to lend you. In this case, bringing in a partner halves your risk and the bank's.

Partnerships

In my experience, the most successful partnerships are those where the two parties have known each other for several years, were at the same dental school, and worked together as associates. If you can achieve this trifecta, the partnership is more likely to be compatible and equitable. You will know the other person's work ethic, the way they interact with staff and patients, their treatment philosophy, and have an idea of how they would manage a clinic.

On the other hand, beware of partnering with a dentist who owns another clinic and works in it part-time. In this case, you would need to question whether they would be more than a silent partner—someone who only makes cameo appearances in return for a share of the profits. You will need someone willing to roll their sleeves up and help you manage the clinic. Will they use their experience to guarantee you greater success than you could achieve as a solo practitioner? Balance your needs with the costs involved in bringing in a partner. If the costs outweigh the financial benefits, go it alone.

> **Purtzki's Law:** Partnerships are often messy and can dissolve during your career. Only seek a partner when necessary.

Let me illustrate: if you need to borrow $800,000 to start your clinic but halve that figure by bringing in a partner, your exposure is $400,000. Assuming a ten-year term at a 5% interest rate, you will save about $4,000 per month. However, when you retire, you are giving up 50% of the equity and profits, along with half of the final selling price of the clinic.

Consider this scenario: commencing in year four, the clinic pays both partners $150,000 annually in profit distribution. If you sell the practice for $1.5 million ten years later, your partner will receive $1.5 million in profit distribution and $750,000 in sales proceeds. That's a cool $2.25 million for a $400,000 investment. If you had chosen to be a solo practitioner, that $2.25 million would have been yours.

Earlier I said that dental start-ups are less risky; unfortunately, this is not the case with dental partnerships because they work differently from other types of business. Take an auto repair shop, for instance. Pat and Sam have complementary skills and feel they have a better chance of success working together, so they go into partnership. Pat is an entrepreneur with a talent for running businesses; he looks after the finances, brings business in, and drives business success. Sam is an excellent mechanic; he completes the repairs efficiently and keeps customers happy. They agree they should only take enough from the business in the early days to pay personal and living expenses. They reinvest the remaining profits in the company. Long-term success is their top priority. Profits are always shared equally regardless of each partner's contribution to the company.

In my experience, dental partnerships are similar but with one significant difference; it's not in a dentist's DNA to share profits based on the percentage of ownership. Dentists are raised on the "eat-what-you-kill" principle. In other words, the dentist partner expects to be remunerated based on the revenues he generates from treating patients. As a result, many dentists insist on operating a cost-sharing arrangement. Under this plan, the dentist providing the service to a patient earns the income from that patient, sharing costs on an agreed formula.

If both dentists focus on treating patients, who is responsible for driving the ship? Someone needs to prioritize building an efficient and profitable practice. Compounding this issue is that few dentists have the skills to manage a clinic, let alone any interest. It is a Herculean task to build a first-class clinic from the ground up. You have to develop management systems from scratch, you need a human resources department to ensure the hiring and retention of top-notch staff, and someone needs to be responsible for developing and implementing a marketing strategy. You cannot expect to open the doors to your clinic and see it run itself successfully. Do not delegate this critical role to an employee. In a corporate environment the Chief Executive Officer (CEO) is responsible for all vital aspects of the business. They ensure profitability and growth, and they are the ultimate decision-maker. If you left this job to two partner dentists in a dental practice, it would take forever to achieve anything.

A start-up dental practice needs one dentist to assume the role of CEO. It is they who handle the business and make all day-to-day decisions. In this case, they should be compensated for lost patient revenues while engaged in bigger-picture practice business.

Selecting a Suitable Partner

How do you choose a partner with whom you are compatible? What criteria should you use? To begin with, it takes a lot more than a positive gut feeling and a vague notion of compatibility. Here's a checklist of questions you should ask yourself.

- How well do they relate to patients and staff? Check their references.

- How much dentistry are they able to produce? High producers are critical to a successful practice with high volume and low overhead.

- Are you compatible? Compatibility isn't always easy to define; for a start, you shouldn't base it on the fact that you enjoy a beer or a glass of wine together socially. Consider compatibility testing by a professional.

- Do they display good leadership skills? Do they acknowledge and support staff members in achieving the clinic's and your personal goals?

- Do they project a professional image?

- Are they likable, interesting, or pleasant to be around? Are people comfortable around them? Do they have a positive attitude?

An Example Contract

In the following partnership agreement example, I have used the solo group model as the business structure. I urge you to discuss the best legal arrangement for your particular circumstances with your lawyer. The solo group model is popular because it provides autonomy for each partner. Think of the contract as a prenuptial agreement. It will outline how revenue and expenses are shared and how either party can exit the relationship should the need arise.

The Revenue and Cost-Sharing Arrangement

Doctor revenues. Each dentist is entitled to 100% of the professional fees they generate from treating their patients.

Hygiene revenues. Each dentist is entitled to the hygiene revenues from patients assigned to their respective practice.

Hygiene expenses. Each dentist is responsible for the pro-rata costs of the salaries of all hygienists, based on monthly hygiene revenue attributable to patients assigned to each dentist.

Associate revenues. Should the partners jointly decide to engage an associate dentist, the partners will mutually determine the terms of engagement. Revenue generated from the associate's services will be divided equally by the dentists unless otherwise mutually agreed. Typically, 40% of the associate's revenues belong to the associate, and the remaining 60% is split equally between the dentists.

Shared expenses. *Note: As it is a production-based expense, this clause mainly concerns dental supplies.*

Each partner will contribute to the cost of the dental supplies proportionate to their respective collections revenue. The partners will contribute equally to shared expenses other than dental supplies.

Practice hours. The partners will jointly determine a calendar for each dentist's clinic hours. Both parties will do their best to ensure that each receives equal access to the premises.

Patient allocation. New patients to the practice will be equitably allocated. Patients requesting the services of a specific dentist will be referred to that dentist, with the understanding that patients who do not ask to see a particular dentist will be assigned in such a way as to equalize the total number of new patients assigned to each dentist.

Vacation time. The partners agree to provide as much notice as possible for planned absences to ensure continued patient care and smooth scheduling.

Note: This is particularly important with start-ups. A clause could also be added to state that each dentist will supervise the other dentist's practice during holidays or absences for up to 100 hours per year.

Short-term disability. If a partner is disabled for a period of time, not exceeding six weeks, the remaining dentist agrees to provide clinical care to the disabled dentist's patients for up to ten hours per week at no cost to the disabled dentist and perform all necessary hygiene checks.

The Buy-Sell Agreement

There should always be an agreed-upon exit strategy that ensures a smooth transition when entering into a legal relationship. A buy-sell agreement is a tool used to achieve this outcome. This agreement minimizes the chance of either party leaving on bad terms. Consider it a way of protecting the financial nest you have worked so hard to build. It is highly likely that, at some point, you will use this agreement to plan your exit from the business.

Do not use a boilerplate document; it will only mirror the standardized solutions of others. I strongly advise you and your partner to work with a lawyer to tailor the agreement to meet your needs.

Here is a brief look at the primary parts of a buy-sell agreement. You should amend any buy-sell agreement to meet your needs and cover anything else related to your specific situation.

Restrictions on Transfer

A restriction on transfer prevents one partner from selling or transferring their interest in the practice without the agreement of the other partner.

Sales to Third Party

If a sale is agreed upon, you need a clause stating that no partner shall sell their interest to a third party unless the third party has agreed with the remaining dentist that the existing cost-sharing and buy-sell agreements would bind the third party.

Right of First Refusal to Purchase

There are two basic types of right of first refusal:

The selling partner must obtain a third-party offer

In this situation, the seller solicits a bona fide third-party offer. In most circumstances the offer must be cash and unconditional. The seller then gives notice to the remaining dentist and offers them an opportunity to purchase the selling partner's share of the practice on the same terms and conditions as the third-party offer. If the remaining partner rejects the offer, the selling dentist is free to sell their share of the practice to the third party.

There are challenges to this type of right of first refusal. Potential buyers may be unwilling to incur the time and cost of preparing such an unconditional offer. It puts the remaining partner in a strong position. They have the luxury of waiting until an offer is on the table and don't need to spend time, money, and energy on a buy-out plan.

The seller notifies the remaining dentist first

In this situation, the selling partner presents their terms and conditions for selling their interest in the practice to the remaining dentist, who is free to accept or reject the offer. Should they reject the offer, the seller is free to sell to a third party within a prescribed period. However, the terms and conditions of the offer cannot be more favorable to the third party than the offer made to the remaining dentist.

This version favors the seller because they do not need to find a purchaser first. Rejecting the offer is a risky proposition for the remaining dentist. They have no idea who the new dentist will be; a new partner can be simply thrust upon them.

Restrictive Covenant

The selling partner agrees to the usual restrictive covenants regarding practicing within a specific geographic radius and the solicitation of patients and employees. This protects the remaining dentist from his ex-partner setting up in direct competition.

Mandatory Withdrawal

Suppose one partner receives a license suspension or acts in a manner that results in the practice suffering an unacceptable hit to its reputation in the dental community. In that case, the departing dentist will be required to sell the practice to the other dentist. The purchase price will be discounted by fifty percent, based on a fair-market valuation, and must be paid within sixty days.

Buy/Sell on Death

In the case of the death of a cost-share partner, the purchase price of the practice must be paid in full by the remaining dentist. A compulsory buy-out upon death clause is crucial to avoid burdening the deceased's estate with a dental clinic that has no marketable value.

If a surviving partner can't afford the buy-out, it can cause multiple problems, including patient attrition—which can be extensive and rapid when a dentist dies. The buy-sell agreement should include a funding mechanism to provide cash in the case of the death of a partner. One way to achieve this is to purchase life insurance for each dentist with the other partner named as the beneficiary. The amount of life insurance purchased can be agreed upon by the partners in advance as a reasonable buy-out price in the case of death, or a practice valuation can determine it.

Suppose the partners choose not to purchase life insurance. In that case, an alternative could be an agreement to gradually pay out the value of the deceased dentist's interest in the clinic to their estate, in monthly installments, for a year starting from the date of death.

Buy/Sell and Long-Term Disability

Suppose a dentist becomes disabled for more than a year. The remaining dentist must purchase the disabled dentist's practice at a ten percent discount based on practice valuation, to be paid in monthly installments over an agreed period (usually six to twelve months). The parties may arrange for a disability buy-out insurance policy. However, most practitioners don't do this because insurance policies can be prohibitively expensive.

Termination

A termination clause ensures that the agreement is automatically terminated under the following circumstances:

- If either party goes into bankruptcy or proposes to its creditors.
- If either party dies or becomes disabled for more than one year.
- If the parties agree in writing to the termination of the agreement.

5

The Business Plan

Successful entrepreneurs always begin a new venture with a rigorous examination of their business plan, but writing one is an unfamiliar concept for most dentists who wish to start their dental practice and open a clinic. However, as the dental market becomes more competitive and the capital required to build a clinic increases, lenders insist on a detailed business plan as a condition for loan approval. The business plan is much more than a document for your banker. It is a compass showing you true north, ensuring you stay on track, meet, and hopefully exceed your goals.

> **Purtzki's Law:** A good business plan is the foundation of a successful career. Time spent on developing a sound plan is time well spent.

A business plan is a dynamic document that requires updating as more information becomes available. The value of doing a business plan is not so much in the finished document (although if you are going to present it to a bank manager, it becomes a vital component of the loan application) but in the process of pulling it together. To write a business plan, you must conduct considerable research and answer hundreds of questions relevant to your business idea. A business plan ensures no nasty surprises waiting for you when you start your practice. While the bank will not require everything listed below, a comprehensive business plan is an asset to your dental practice and increases your chances of success.

Assumptions

When writing a business plan, one of the most challenging things is making assumptions. Assumptions are educated guesses as to what a situation is or might be. Many people find that making assumptions is the main stumbling block to developing their plan. The secret is that it doesn't matter too much if your assumptions are wrong. Most of your assumptions will be inaccurate at first. Few of us can look into the future and predict what will happen. Assumptions are guidelines from which to work. They allow us to see whether things are better or worse than we thought they would be over a given period. Once we have these guidelines, we can change our assumptions every time we get new information.

Don't be afraid to make assumptions. You can update and refine them as more information becomes available or circumstances change. Research them, test them, play with them, do what you like with them but MAKE them!

At the end of this chapter, I will provide an outline business plan for *Scratch Start Dental*, owned by Dr. A. Dente. But first, I'll give you a crash tour of the elements of a typical business plan.

Table of Contents

A table of contents (TOC) makes it easier for people (including you) to read and refer to your business plan.

Executive Summary

The Executive Summary is written last but appears at the beginning of the business plan and is one of the most critical sections. It gives the reader an outline, or snapshot, of your business. Bankers tend to read business plans the same way. First, they read the executive summary, review the cash flow to see if the project makes financial sense, and then check whether the owner and management team have the necessary skill and experience.

The Mission Statement

A mission statement is a short paragraph or two that clearly states the scope of your services and your practice philosophy. Everything in a company grows out of its mission statement, from its behavior to its strategic planning and decision-making model. A mission statement sets the tone for the clinic, provides it with focus, and gives employees something to live up to.

Scope of Service

The executive summary is not the place to give masses of details about your service. All that is required are one or two paragraphs that tell the reader a little about your practice model. In the case of your clinic, you may want to mention that you will be providing hygiene and any other specialist services. Do you have a USP (Unique Selling Proposition)? Is there anything that will make you stand out?

Financial Highlights

Gross Revenue: Show your total projected practice revenues for the financial years covered by the plan. Leave the breakdown between general dentistry and hygiene for the section on finances.

Net Income: Show the practice's net operating income; that is, your gross revenues minus all direct expenses. At this stage, and for the business plan, you need not consider taxes.

Owners Investment Cash/Equipment: What is your investment in the practice? List the amount of cash you will put in (this is your opening cash balance and any other money you intend to invest over the first year). Also, list any equipment you will put into the business and total the value (at today's values).

Profit: What month do you expect your practice to produce a positive net cash flow? Mention how you will service the debt and still have enough money to survive. Show how much you expect to earn as a part-time associate after opening your clinic. Demonstrate that you have sufficient start-up capital. Show when you will start repaying the debt.

Market Sector

In this section, mention anything relevant to your target market. Perhaps you plan to open a dental clinic that treats children, or targets people requiring advanced procedures or cosmetic dentistry?

Discuss the size of your market and the percentage you plan to capture. For example, maybe you plan to open your clinic in a particular neighborhood because of a building boom. If you are close to a new development, how many properties is the developer constructing? Over what period? How many people will be moving into those homes?

Look into the future a little; will new technology change your market? Will changing demographics increase, decrease, or change your customer base? Will local, national, and global changes to the economy affect you? If so, how?

Customers (aka Patients)

The more you understand your potential patients, the more likely you will attract them to your clinic. Describe your ideal new patient. Are you looking for newcomers to the area, or do you have plans to attract them to your clinic from another dentist's clinic? If so, how?

Consider your typical patients: are they young, middle-aged, old, or of all ages? Are they predominately male or female? Are they mostly, or exclusively, business people, sports lovers, mothers, fathers, business owners, managers, directors, employed, unemployed, school children, car owners, etc.? Are they fit, trying to lose weight, retired, cyclists, or environmentalists?

Where do your potential patients live? Is your catchment area confined to your immediate locale, or will you be drawing them from further afield? If you are in a downtown location, will you appeal to people who live or work in the core, or both? Knowing this will help you decide on your opening hours. Where do your patients currently go for dental treatment?

Discovering this information will save you time, money, and a great deal of heartache. It will also show the bank that you are serious about your dental practice and are treating it like any other business.

Competition

Your competition will be any dentist that could provide your potential patients with the exact services you plan to offer. Readers will be looking for you to know the number of competing dentists and their strengths and weaknesses in relation to your clinic. Strengths may include things like how well established they are, their good reputation, their central location, parking availability, and modern facilities.

Weaknesses might be the reverse of their strengths. Because they are well-established, they may be booking appointments further out, the clinic's technology is dated, or there is limited parking.

Consider how your new clinic might offer patients additional services such as better opening hours, a more comfortable reception area, state-of-the-art seats, televisions with headphones in the operatories, or online booking. The latter has become very popular recently.

Note what challenges you might face in the future should another dentist open close to your location. How would you handle that situation?

Services

As mentioned earlier in the market sector section, list the services you plan to offer, especially if you plan to provide more than general dentistry and hygiene. Additional services might include: cosmetic, periodontal, orthodontic, pediatric, endodontic, or prosthodontics.

Promotion

Promotion is vital if patients are going to hear about your new clinic. In the business plan, you should clearly state what promotional activity you will undertake. A mistake made by many people in their business plans is to create a brilliant promotional strategy full of innovative ways of promoting their company, but without allocating sufficient funds to follow through. It is no use trying to impress the reader with an extensive campaign you can't afford. Ground your plan in reality.

Before writing this section, deciding what you can afford to set aside as a promotional budget is a good idea. Once you know your budget, work out how to get maximum exposure for your dollars.

Revenues

Demonstrate how you will convert inquiries into clinic visits and walk-ins into appointments. Plan to have your office manager or another staff member trained and responsible for building the new patient base.

Location and Administration

Provide information on your clinic's physical location. If it is on a busy street mention the number of people who walk by per hour, day, week, etc. If it is on the main bus route, highlight the fact. Detail anything that you think might impress the reader. For example, there is excellent parking, a refreshment area with a coffee bar, and WiFi. Mention anything that will encourage patients to seek you out.

Personnel

Management

Highlight your relevant skills, experience, and attitude to show that you are ready to start your own dental practice. Not all great dentists are good managers; banks want to hear that you will run the practice with the help of a first-rate office management team.

Staff

Provide information on the staff you are going to hire. Include job descriptions and the skills, background, and experience you will be seeking. Banks will look at your staffing plan favorably if you mention that you will be hiring an experienced practice manager.

Financials

A comprehensive business plan should include a break-even analysis, balance sheet, income statement, cash flow spreadsheet, and cash flow projections for years one through three.

The sample business plan below for Scratch Start Dental provides some examples.

Balance Sheet

A Balance Sheet is a snapshot showing the practice's assets, liabilities, and equity at a given point in time.

Cash Flow

In all businesses, cash is king. It doesn't matter how well you are doing in sales or how much profit you are making; if you can't pay your bills, you are in serious trouble. Think of a cash flow spreadsheet as a prediction of your company's chequing account; it predicts the clinic's cash in and out and then shows actual cash in and out each month. A cash flow forecast is an invaluable planning tool and shows readers that you know how much cash you require in hand each month to meet your obligations.

Risk Assessment

What significant risks are you taking by starting this business? How are you going to deal with these problems? What if you sign up fewer patients than expected in the first few months, have difficulty hiring quality staff, new equipment doesn't arrive on schedule, or another dentist opens their doors at the same time? Also, consider risks from positive things that happen. For instance, what happens if you are overwhelmed with new patients, wait times for appointments become too long, and you begin receiving complaints?

When you are writing your business plan, it is the perfect time to look at the risks of starting your dental practice. Don't be tempted to underplay potential problems. Face up to the dangers, recognize them, and have a strategy to deal with them. Those risks will be there whether you face them or not, so it is better to meet problems up front and find ways to deal with them.

If you show the reader that you have identified the risks, assessed them, and dealt with them, you will increase your credibility tenfold. Having a contingency plan for any significant problems you foresee will alleviate many of the concerns of those who read your business plan.

Calculating Break-Even

Break-even revenue means that the revenue generated by the clinic is equal to all fixed and variable expenses. The calculations below relate to the numbers in the spreadsheet in the following sample business plan.

Fixed expenses are those that don't change when revenues increase or decrease. Let's assume you determine that your fixed annual expenditures will be $240,000, including salaries and benefits of $130,000.

Your **variable** expenses are $60,000, equating to 12% of revenues, and include dental supplies and lab fees. The remaining 88% of revenues contributes to paying your fixed expenses. Accountants call this 88% the **Contribution Margin Percentage.**

To calculate the break-even revenue, divide the fixed expenses by the Contribution Margin Percentage. Break-even point = fixed expenses ÷ Contribution Margin Percentage. In the above example, the break-even point would be calculated as $240,000 ÷ .88 = $272,727.

In this case, if the clinic brings in $273,000 in revenues, it will pay for all the running costs, but there is virtually zero profit. In my sample business plan example on page 49, Dr. Dente predicts revenues of $500,000, which are well above break-even.

In dollars and cents, the break-even analysis answers whether or not you should consider starting the clinic. The break-even calculation is an essential tool; it helps you prove the viability of your dental practice.

Critical Steps To-Do List

To-Do Item	Start Date	Completion Date	Comments
Premises lease signed			
Business plan for bank			
Search for interior designer			
Get bids from contractors			
Hire office mgr./ front desk			
Arrange for insurance			
Set up the legal entity			
Dental equipment quotes			
Advertise for staff			
Interview staff			
Set up website			
Business systems set up			
Hire staff			
Staff training			
Advertising for an open house			
Open clinic			

Sample Business Plan: Scratch Start Dental

The previous pages detailed many things you should consider when starting your dental practice. Your bank's loan officer may not require such an extensive business plan, so here is a sample of what a bare-bones plan might contain:

Title Page

The title page should contain the following information:

- Practice Name
- Contact Name (and address if different from the business)
- Clinic Address
- Clinic Phone Number
- E-mail Address
- Web URL
- Date

Executive Summary

After working seven years as an associate, Dr. Dente has decided to open her own clinic. She has leased a new retail space of 1,900 sq. ft., accommodating six operatories.

To be completed as described at the beginning of this chapter.

Keys to Success

Mission 1: To create a unique full-service dental clinic that will bring in an average of fifty new patients per month. This will be achieved through superior performance, word-of-mouth referrals, and a carefully considered and professional marketing plan.

Mission 2: To optimize the capacity ratio in a modern, accessible, state-of-the-art environment that will provide dentistry seven days a week.

Patient focus: A human resources strategy will be employed to ensure the hiring of committed personnel who exhibit an extraordinary ability to communicate with patients. All staff members will undergo continuous training and regular evaluation to ensure exceptional customer service to patients.

Convenient hours: The clinic will open non-traditional hours, for example on Sundays and every Saturday.

Strategic location: The clinic's location is at a newly developed mixed-use condominium with strong anchor tenants. It enjoys high street exposure to vehicular and pedestrian traffic. It is also situated adjacent to numerous apartment blocks.

Marketing and promotion: We will be launching a professionally designed website within the next few weeks. An extensive social media plan will ensure ongoing exposure to potential patients. We will undertake a direct mail campaign, internal marketing, and community involvement. We will be retaining the services of several consultants to assist with developing a high-profile, modern brand and implementing a comprehensive marketing program.

Home town advantage: Dr. Dente grew up in the community; as such, she has an extensive network of friends and family in the region who will support the clinic.

Patients from previous practice: Dr. Dente works as an associate for another dental office. However, as she is outside of the area designated by the restrictive covenant from her associate work, it is likely that many of her previous patients will gradually follow her to the new clinic once it opens.

Part-time associateship: Dr. Dente will continue to work as an associate as she grows her practice and transitions to full-time at the new location.

Contribution by mentors: Dr. Dente enjoys the support of two experienced business mentors who will consult with her on the effective day-to-day operation of a professional clinic. Working with them, she will ensure patients receive top-quality dental care and that the practice operates to the highest ethical standards.

Lease Summary

Area	1,900 sq. ft.
Parking	Five spaces
Term	Ten years with options to renew for two terms of five years each
Tenant Inducement	$40 per sq. ft.
Basic Rent	$30 per sq. ft. for the first three years, increasing by $1.00 per sq. ft. each year after that
Operating costs	Estimated $15 per sq. ft.
Rent Deposit	Initial deposit $20,000
Exclusivity	Yes
Assignment	Landlord approval is not required if an assignment is to another dentist

Cash Flow Projections: Years 1-3

CASH FLOW PROJECTION FOR YEAR 1-3

	Year 1	Year 2	Year 3
Revenue	$ 500,000	$ 800,000	$ 1,200,000
Expenses			
Fixed expenses	$ 240,000	$ 310,000	$ 410,000
Variable expenses			
Dental supplies	$ 30,000	$ 40,000	$ 50,000
Lab fees	$ 30,000	$ 50,000	$ 80,000
Sub-Total	$ 60,000	$ 90,000	$ 130,000
Total expenses	$ 300,000	$ 400,000	$ 540,000
Operating cash flow	$ 200,000	$ 400,000	$ 660,000
Break-even point	$ 272,000	$ 348,000	$ 460,000

In the spreadsheet above, we predict year one revenues of $500,000. In this scenario, income would need to decline by 46% to ($272,000) before the clinic reaches a break-even point, providing a significant buffer. In year two, predicted revenues of $800,000 would need to decrease by 57% (to $348,000) to reach the break-even point. Year three shows revenues of $1.2 million. In this case, revenues would have to drop by 62% (to $460,000) to reach the break-even point. Operational efficiencies, resulting in an overhead of under 50%, account for the low break-even points shown.

Marketing Strategy

As shown below, we have a seven-point marketing strategy to ensure the clinic achieves the necessary exposure to bring enough patients through the doors to achieve the predicted revenues.

Extended Hours

Dr. Dente will open seven days a week from 9 am to 5 pm to encourage people to check out the new clinic. No dentist nearby offers such flexible hours for residents and people commuting to the community for work.

Website and Social Media

The clinic will have a custom-designed website for better search engine optimization. A social media strategy and implementation plan will ensure regular blogs on popular social media sites such as Facebook, Instagram, and Twitter. The clinic manager will be responsible for posting instructional and informative videos on dental hygiene and other related topics on the clinic's YouTube channel. We believe a strong internet presence is essential to drive new patients to the clinic.

Direct Mail

We will carry out a direct mail campaign in the immediate vicinity of the clinic. Recent research has indicated that this cost-effective advertising medium often outperforms trendier methods of promoting dental clinics.

Community Involvement

The clinic will be active in the community, including both the business community and the general public. The practice will join and be an active member of the local chamber of commerce, support community events, and sponsor local clubs, youth organizations, and sports teams (e.g., supplying high-quality mouthguards). Staff will participate in community education, including speaking at schools, retirement homes, and other local groups.

Team Training and Development

Employees will undergo formal training in all aspects of working in a dental clinic. Training will include technical development to keep abreast of current trends, technology, and soft skills training—particularly in delivering exceptional customer service.

Internal Marketing

We believe every employee has a role in guaranteeing a positive patient experience. Word-of-mouth referrals are essential to the early growth of the practice, and it is a critical plank in the clinic's marketing strategy that will ensure the clinic develops a high profile in the community.

Branding

Dr. Dente understands the need for branding and has retained the services of a marketing company to identify the clinic's brand promise and help build a strong brand. Strategies include team uniforms featuring the professionally designed clinic logo, and impactful signage on the building's street-facing exterior. The brand will appear everywhere there is patient interaction. Consistency and professionalism will underscore every aspect of the dental practice.

Cash Flow Projection—Years 1 to 3

CASH FLOW PROJECTION FOR YEAR 1-3	Year 1	Year 2	Year 3
Revenue	$ 500,000	$ 800,000	$ 1,200,000
Expenses			
Fixed expenses			
Accounting/Professional fees	$ 4,000	$ 6,000	$ 10,000
Advertising and promotion	22,000	25,000	30,000
Bank charges	4,000	6,000	8,000
Insurance	5,000	6,000	7,000
Office	18,000	25,000	40,000
Rent	50,000	50,000	50,000
Telephone/Utilities	7,000	12,000	15,000
Salaries and benefits	130,000	180,000	250,000
Sub-Total	$ 240,000	$ 310,000	$ 410,000
Variable expenses			
Dental supplies	$ 30,000	$ 40,000	$ 50,000
Lab fees	30,000	50,000	80,000
Sub-Total	$ 60,000	$ 90,000	$ 130,000
Total expenses	$ 300,000	$ 400,000	$ 540,000
Operating cash flow	$ 200,000	$ 400,000	$ 660,000

Opening Balance Sheet

Opening Balance Sheet		
Assets		
Cash		$ 100,000
Start up costs-budget		100,000
Leaseholds		400,000
Equipment		400,000
		$ 1,000,000
Liabilities		
Bank Loan		$ 1,000,000

6

Arranging Bank Financing

For the average person, getting a bank loan for a business start-up is almost futile. Banks require excellent credit scores, collateral, personal guarantees, and proof that the company will do enough business to repay the loan. The chances are that banks will show you the door unless you have some serious skin in the game. Unless, that is, you are a dentist. Banks love lending money to dentists and will roll out the red carpet when you apply for that $1 million loan to start your clinic. Choose the right bank to partner with, and you'll have to jump over very few hurdles to get the money.

Surprised? Don't be. Banks are not altruistic; they know there is strong demand for dental care and that dentists are high income-earners who are not subject to the vagaries of the economy. Bankruptcy rates and defaults on loans are very low in the industry. You are a safe bet in terms of lending money.

Bankers are long-term thinkers. They know the value of having a dentist as a loyal client. They will be keen to service your needs and help you transition from an associate to a practice owner. In return, they plan to capitalize on their relationship with you over the years: think mortgages on fancy homes and loans for luxury cars. Once you have repaid the loans, the bank's investment arm will be there to help you build your retirement portfolio.

Case Study

Cooper Leighton has been an associate for three years. He works at a busy clinic in the heart of a thriving city. At thirty, Cooper feels he has done his time and is ready to open his own clinic. Life has been good; he is an avid paddleboarder, an active community volunteer, and coaches a local football team. He plans to marry within the year and wants to start a family. He has been planning to strike out independently for a while and recently spotted a perfect location. His lease offer on the property was accepted subject to financing, so he now has three weeks to secure funding. Like most associates, he has no savings and a student loan of $200,000. Cooper is analytical and has labored over budgets for his new clinic. He needs a $1 million loan, $800,000 to finance the leasehold improvements and equipment, and $200,000 for the operating line of credit.

Understanding the need for a sound business plan, budgets, and financial projections, he presented the bank with extensive documentation. They approved the loan, waiving the need for collateral or guarantees from family members. Not only that, the bank offered him the loan at its prime rate (usually reserved for VIP clients) and deferred repayments for two years.

To put this into perspective, Cooper has zero experience setting up and running a dental clinic. Surprisingly, this is all true, and many of my clients have had the same or similar experiences. If banks have this much faith in new dentists, then you can overcome any trepidation in opening your own clinic.

If all that sounds a little too easy, you are not wrong. Banks don't simply hand out a million dollars without a ton of due diligence. As we saw in Chapter Five, you need a comprehensive business plan and all your ducks in a row before approaching a bank. However, as a dentist-entrepreneur, you are in a privileged position, unlike someone trying to get a loan to open a retail store next door to your clinic. Chances are they've received the cold shoulder from several banks, and even if they managed to secure a loan, they would have had to provide overwhelming security and personal guarantees. Generally, banks only seem to lend money to people who don't need it.

A word of warning. Not all banks will welcome you with open arms and make things easy; you must search for one that is familiar with the dental industry and specializes in financing dentists. These institutions are more likely to give you generous loan conditions and quick approval. The latter is crucial if you are sitting on an accepted lease offer with a deadline to arrange financing.

Create a shortlist of banks that fit these criteria and make appointments with their loan managers to discuss your needs and confirm their interest in supporting your application and the broad scope of the terms. You will likely discover that their terms are all similar.

When you meet with a loan officer, don't wander in for a casual conversation about your needs—be prepared and professional. First impressions are crucial, so take along a one-page loan proposal. Doing this forces you to consider your loan needs and ability to service the loan. This document should outline the terms you are expecting. If you miss this first step, you put the loan manager in the driving seat, and they may try to impose less-than-ideal lending conditions on you.

A pro tip in dealing with banks on your shortlist is not to ask each one to prepare a formal, binding commitment letter. These letters take a lot of the banker's time, and if they are not aware that you are soliciting letters from other banks, they will be upset if you choose to go with another bank. I call this taking the scorched-earth approach. Choose the bank whose terms and conditions you like best and move forward with them alone. This approach will protect your relationship with the other banks should you need their support in the future.

Sample One-Page Loan Request

The following outlines the basic information required in your one-page loan request. Remember, this is a starting point only; you will be expected to provide significant additional information as outlined below.

Dr. Dente (Acme Dental Practice)

Proposal submitted: (Date)
Borrower: Dr. Dente Inc.
Financing required:

Demand loan: $800,000 (Leaseholds and Equipment)

- Approval required by: xxxx/xx/xx.

- Loan amortization: ten years, repayable at any time without penalty

- Repayments are to commence in year three.

- Interest rate: preferred customer rate (e.g., bank prime).

Line of credit: $150,000 (Working Capital).

- Interest rate: bank prime.

Security

- All practice assets, including accounts receivable.
- Dr. Dente's personal guarantee. A spousal guarantee is not available.

Attachments

- Personal statement of net worth
- Practice and personal cash flow projections
- Quote from equipment seller and building contractor

Information Required by Banks

Banks request similar information from dentists looking for practice financing, and almost all offer templates to assist you in providing all the relevant information they require. There are five key pieces banks will need from you:

1. Business plan
2. Three-year financial projections
3. Your last two years' tax returns and financial statements showing your associate income
4. Your net worth statement, using the bank's template
5. A signed lease offer

Negotiation Tips

Assuming you have carefully created your budgets, don't accept a loan that doesn't meet your financial needs. It's tempting to take what's on offer and go back for more later. This approach is a fool's errand; banks hate it when you do an Oliver and go back, cap in hand, saying, "Please, sir, can I have some more?" As with Dickens's Oliver Twist, it won't go well. If you need $800,000 to build your clinic and the bank is only willing to give you $700,000, do not compromise. Life can get ugly quickly when you don't have enough operating capital to pay for dental supplies and salaries.

> **Purtzki's Law:** Never accept less money from the bank than you need. It is almost impossible to go back for more.

On the other side of the equation, don't ask for or take more than you need. In those early halcyon days, it feels like free money, but remember, you have to pay it back—with interest. Trim your budget wherever possible; a $100,000 reduction in your construction budget means, factoring in interest, $130,000 less you will have to pay back.

Look at ways to save money; if that is not your forte, find someone who loves to be thrifty and put them in charge of finding ways to pare down the budget. Get comparative quotes from all contractors and designers. Shop around for deals on equipment, and don't buy top-of-the-range unless there is an overwhelming reason to do so—your patients won't know a top brand name dental chair from a less expensive name. Look for deals, last year's models, and even used equipment from reliable sources—this can save you significant sums of money and reduce the time it takes you to repay the loan.

> **Purtzki's Law:** Don't blow your budget on expensive equipment. Patients don't care what brand you have.

If you are leasing space that allows for six operatories, consider equipping only three and adding the equipment to the others later. An added advantage is that you can purchase more up-to-date equipment when the time comes.

Don't forget the sales taxes you will have to pay on all the leasehold improvements and equipment. Banks will not finance sales taxes. For example, if your budget is $800,000, there will be an additional $96,000 in taxes to pay (assuming a 12% sales tax in your jurisdiction). You should address the tax issue as part of the loan application; for instance, you might ask for a larger line of credit to cover the sales taxes. I am always surprised at how silent bankers can be on sales taxes.

One option to potentially skirt the sales tax challenge is to get your dental CPA to outline the tax advantages of leasing versus purchasing. Usually, the lease option includes the financing of sales taxes.

The Bank's Commitment Letter

Don't get too excited when you receive a letter of commitment from your bank. I have had many clients whose initial euphoria quickly dissipated once they had a chance to read the fine print. Never accept a loan before receiving and reviewing the bank's commitment letter. The last thing you want is to sign a loan agreement where the details have changed as it was processed.

It is always the borrower's responsibility to fully understand the loan terms. To my knowledge, a banker has never accepted fault for a "miscommunication" regarding the loan terms. You may trust your account manager and the promises they make, but any terms they agree to have the potential of being altered by their superiors. Without a commitment letter, the first time you might learn about critical changes or amendments to the loan is on the date of signing. At that point, your options are limited. For example, if you suddenly discover the bank is now demanding personal guarantees from you and your spouse, there may be no time to secure an alternative lending source.

A typical bank commitment letter contains the following elements:

- Loan amount
- Interest rate
- Repayment requirements
- Security required
- Loan conditions, e.g., maintaining specific working capital and debt-to-equity ratios, restrictions on distributions of profits to owners, and reporting requirements
- Legal and commitment fees

Don't let the commitment letter faze you; it is not written in stone. Treat it as an opening salvo and negotiate where possible, particularly in areas such as the security required and bank fees. For instance, banks often try to pass bank fees off as standard or policy, as if they can't possibly waive them. Ignore their bluster; many of my clients have negotiated these fees to an absolute minimum. Everything is negotiable if the bank wants the business.

Negotiating with a bank is not something most dentists are comfortable doing, so consider hiring someone knowledgeable about how banks and account managers think. For example, a dental practice start-up consultant has the expertise to handle bank negotiations successfully and has no fear of bargaining hard on behalf of their clients.

7

Your Dental Office— Design and Construction

One of the significant advantages of starting your own practice and designing your clinic is that you can create everything from scratch. This is your opportunity to build the functionality, efficiency, comfort, and ambiance you need to help you stand out from every other dentist in your locale.

In the past, clinic design focused on the needs of dentists and their staff. As long as the patient had a chair to sit on, some old magazines to flip through, and the place was clean, they wouldn't complain. Demand for dental treatment exceeded supply, much like the current situation where we have a global shortage of doctors.

Fast forward to today, and there are almost as many dental clinics in town as coffee shops. However, many of them sport decades-old designs and layouts. They look tired, overcrowded, and have an unpleasant medical clinic vibe. When I talk to dentists, one out of three is unhappy with the layout and design of their clinic. These progressive individuals realize that patients judge their professionalism and competency by how they interact with the clinic and its atmosphere. Investment in clinic renovation is growing, but it's costly.

Design as a Competitive Edge

You, however, are uniquely positioned to get it right from the outset. Having a well-designed, welcoming clinic will help you bring in patients quickly. Sterile, medical-centric clinics are no longer acceptable if you want to have a thriving practice. The aim should be to provide a soothing, comforting environment that communicates the quality of your dentistry and customer service. In recent years, dental patients have become increasingly discerning. They expect high standards and are not slow to switch dentists to find a state-of-the-art, modern dental practice.

A carefully orchestrated space gives patients an idea of the level of dental care they will receive. Imagine visiting a dentist for the first time where the waiting room carpets are stained, the chairs uncomfortable, and the receptionist is hidden behind a high counter. You'd be forgiven for thinking the dentist and hygienists might be using outdated equipment and that your overall experience might not be as pleasant as you had hoped.

In contrast, imagine you pop by to check out a new dentist in town. As you walk into the office, you notice a waiting room flooded with natural light; the walls are brightly painted and adorned with tasteful art, light orchestral music is playing, and the smell of freshly brewed coffee greets you along with a warm welcome by a staff member. How would you feel? I suggest you would immediately be sold on making this your new clinic.

Get the design element of your new clinic right, and it will become an excellent advertising tool. Impressed patients talk to friends and family and will actively recommend you. I work with dentists for a living and often speak to patients to see what they like about a practice. Inevitably, they talk about wait times, friendly, courteous staff, décor, ambiance, and whether the place is soothing—they never tell me how efficient the dentist was in inserting a crown.

> **Purtzki's Law:** Women usually select the family dentist; design with them in mind. And, never underestimate the power of good clinic design to attract patients.

I remember assisting an associate in building their new clinic a year or so ago and recall how amazed he was at how many new patients he was attracting via his website. When asked, they readily told his staff that the stunning photographs of the clinic made them want to check him out.

Effective Design Improves Productivity

Leading edge clinic design is not only an essential tool for attracting new patients, but it also improves the efficiency and productivity of your practice. Consider employee and patient flow when working with your architect and designer. It's surprising how much more pleasant life will be when employees can move around without bumping into each other or patients. It also means you will treat patients quicker, increasing your turnover rate. Your goal should be to create a pleasant experience for staff and patients.

Design—Don't Lose Control

In my experience, most dentists prepare a rough sketch of how they'd like to see the clinic laid out and show it to their construction company's dental office designer or an equipment company. They then provide input and working drawings. It's at this stage that things can begin to go off track. Most construction companies focus on functionality and not aesthetics. It's crucial to ensure your intended aesthetic considerations are not lost when these well-intended professionals become involved.

Your goal should be to design and build a clinic that impresses not only the competition but potential patients and employees too. Get it right, and high-performing hygienists and other employees will knock on your door, wanting to join your practice. You are a dentist, not an architect, so you will need to retain the services of the best dental practice designer you can find. Ask around, search the internet, and when you find a candidate do your due diligence; check their references and visit the clinics they have designed.

Get it right, and you will have a clinic that still looks modern, functions well, and has a great atmosphere twenty years later. The secret is not to compromise when you first start out; your investment will pay dividends in the future when you decide to sell.

Good design and lousy design cost the same, so you might as well do it right the first time.

Technology

We are in the middle of the fourth industrial revolution. Technology is moving at an unprecedented pace; it is challenging to keep up, but purchasing anything that isn't state-of-the-art will prove to be a false economy. The more "toys" you have that allow you to provide the most current treatment and care, the better edge you will have over your competition. For example, you might have the latest scheduling and appointment software, 3D radiography, or the use of artificial intelligence. When designing your space, ensure it will allow for future technological advances. A little research into what's coming down the pipeline in terms of cool new gadgets and equipment, and making your clinic technology friendly, could allow you to keep ahead of the competition way into the future.

COVID is not going away; it is a new reality. Design your space with social distancing in mind; plan for larger waiting rooms and operatories to allow space for patients and staff to move around freely.

Intelligent, forward-thinking design is a critical part of practice success. Why?

- Patients increasingly demand a more comfortable and soothing environment.

- Modern, upbeat, comfortable clinics increase patient referrals and drive new patients via the practice website.

- State-of-the-art design sets you apart from the vanilla clinics in your neighborhood.

- An ultra-modern clinic demonstrates how much you value your patients.

- Intelligent design reduces stress, making the workplace a healthier environment.

- Well-thought-out clinic design increases efficiency and productivity.

Construction

Let's follow two dentists using different construction models to plan their clinic build. First, we have traditional Joe, who plans to use the **design-bid-build model**. Joe has a friend who manages public projects; this is the method he uses to keep costs down. Joe hires an architect to create the construction blueprints, an interior designer to handle the color palette, furnishings and fittings, and a contractor to make it all happen.

A few weeks later, the plans for his new clinic are ready for inspection. With a few tweaks, Joe approves them and begins the construction phase. He reaches out to three construction firms experienced in building dental clinics and asks them to quote on the job.

In due course, the quotes arrive, and he selects the contractor who submitted the lowest bid. Joe meets with his contractor regularly but soon discovers that the individual sub-contractors are not all working happily together. They are not in sync with timing or interpreting the designer's plans. The contractor has had difficulty keeping them on track because they move forward and do the job as outlined, even when something doesn't make sense or conflicts with another tradespersons' work. The contractor has already given Joe some change orders, and Joe is concerned about keeping to his budget.

Samantha has also secured a lease on an excellent property and needs to begin the design process. She asked a few successful dentist friends how they approached the construction phase, and they suggested the **design-build method**. They explained that, unlike the design-bid-build method, Samantha would choose a specialist firm with architects, interior designers, and dental construction experts. This integrated approach would significantly shorten the construction timeline.

Samantha talked to a few firms and was impressed that using this method ensured that the design and constructability went hand-in-hand. Using this approach meant she was less likely to reach a point where a desired design element was not feasible.

The Pros and Cons of the Design-Build Method

Pros

- There is no need to get competitive bids on each element of the design and construction phase.

- Progress from stage to stage is seamless, and construction can begin during the design phase, saving considerable time. You have a team working for you, not individual, independent sub-trades.

- The construction and design team members talk to each other and can address building challenges as they arise.

- Because design-build firms are responsible for the design process, you can expect fewer change orders.

- With engineering and pre-construction work concurrent with design, you can expect to cut the project timeline by more than one-third.

- Although not the least expensive method, costs are easier to predict, and the contractor can provide a budget close to the final price.

Cons

- It is more challenging to get a competitive price without a bidding process. With the design-build method, you will have to choose your design-build firm before work commences on design. Using this method makes shopping based on price alone almost impossible. It is therefore critical you select a firm with an outstanding reputation.

- As the project owner, you play a significant role in the design and planning stages, but once construction is underway your contractor will make most of the decisions, calling on you on an as-needed basis.

Change Orders

Change orders can be a major headache and mess up your budget. Some changes to your best-laid plans are inevitable and legitimate. Cost increases for products are a fact of life. Supply chain issues can result in swapping one fixture for another which is costlier, or you may discover you can no longer install them without making alterations.

Be wary, however, of unbudgeted cost increases that appear unexpectedly. I have encountered cases where dentists have used the design-bid-build method, and one of the bidders missed out on items when budgeting. These items were then added back as change orders once construction was underway.

When I spoke to dentists who have constructed or remodeled a clinic about whether they would use the same contractor again, more than half told me no, they would not use them again. The reason they give is unwarranted cost increases and construction delays.

Discuss with your contractor precisely how they will handle change orders. The critical thing is that you should approve all change orders in writing to ensure there are no surprises when you receive the invoice.

Tips for Selecting a Building Contractor

- Get recommendations from colleagues. Follow up with them and visit the clinics if possible.

- Find someone with building experience to accompany you when checking out the quality of a contractor's work.

- Inquire about change orders. For example, are change orders at cost or cost plus markup?

- Check whether the contractor has a good reputation for meeting deadlines. Build-in construction delay penalties if possible. Specify, in detail, deadlines for each stage of construction. Stipulate what types of delay are included and excluded. A delay caused by you or an act of God should be excluded. I urge you to get your lawyer to handle your construction delay penalty clause to ensure it is enforceable.

  - Calculate penalties as a percentage of the original contract price. For example, you might build in a penalty of a quarter of one percent per day, or week, capped at five percent of the total contract price. You could also add a grace period before your contractor starts incurring penalties.

- Discuss with the contractor how many projects they usually handle at one time and ask for assurances that they have enough tradespeople on hand to complete the work by the deadline.

8

Staffing Your Practice

Experienced dental employees are in short supply, and great ones are even harder to find. Look around; even well-established dental clinics are struggling to fill vacant positions. Don't delay working on the human resources component of your practice. As soon as you start building your clinic, begin recruiting.

There is a contradiction here. On the one hand, many established practices are hurting because they can't find staff willing to leave where they are currently working. Still, when you set up independently as an associate, your team might follow you to your new clinic. They may feel stuck in a rut or underappreciated by the current practice owner. Even if they don't follow you, you are probably in a stronger position than you think as far as offering an attractive place to work. People get bored, feel undervalued, and want a new challenge. Don't underestimate the draw for motivated employees to be able to put their "stamp" on a new clinic and help create its culture.

How do you find these driven people? An excellent place to start is to reach out to your dental circle of friends and colleagues; ask them whether they know of any good employees who are dissatisfied with their current position and may be open to jumping ship for the right offer.

Who to Hire First?

A sound HR strategy is crucial to a start-up. One critical decision: should you first hire a dental assistant or an office manager? In my experience, this is where many new practice owners make their first big mistake—they choose to hire a dental assistant. Their rationale is that the dental assistant can double-duty answering the phone and dealing with walk-ins. Good luck with that. You might get away with this approach for a short period. Once you have a few patients though, if your assistant is busy helping you, they will not be able to answer the phone promptly, and walk-ins will be ignored (and will walk back out). If they are answering the phone or dealing with a walk-in, they can't be helping you with a patient in the chair. This situation is unprofessional and unsustainable.

If you want to take a professional approach, it makes sense to make your first hire an office manager. In my experience, this person is the cornerstone of a successful practice. They will help you grow the practice quickly and profitably—assuming you hire the right person, but more about that later. Your office manager is the "director of first impressions," a critical role for a new clinic. They will initially assume the receptionist role, handling all front-of-house responsibilities, present a professional image, and begin building client relationships.

Before you start advertising and putting the word out that you are looking for an office manager, sit down and prepare a job description. This document summarizes the tasks they will carry out and your overall expectations for the role. How else will you know what you are looking for in a candidate?

However, before you do this, take a step back and consider what skills you have and what skills might be available from friends and family. For instance, if you know someone who is a social media guru, then maybe they'll help you in the early days of your start-up. When it comes to marketing, at least at the beginning, you are the best person to promote your new practice. Or, perhaps, your spouse is a bookkeeper or accountant? Finding someone who excels in all aspects of operating a practice will be almost impossible. However, utilizing "free" help may reduce the number of skills you need in an office manager.

Here are a few essential responsibilities an office manager should undertake:

- Manage the day-to-day operations of the practice
- Handle the clinic's accounts and ensure all treatments are billed and collected*
- Manage staff
- Recruit employees

- Orient new staff and handle training

- Scheduling

- Help you develop a solid organizational culture

- Market the clinic and monitor social media

*Ideally, the office manager will handle all phases of the accounts receivable, including following up on insurance claims, preparing bank deposits, and ensuring disbursements are made based on invoices or services received.

When interviewing a candidate for the office manager position, don't get hung up on the fact they don't have every skill you need. For example, perhaps they are not comfortable working with accounting software. If this is the case, delegate this task to a bookkeeper.

Salary is another stumbling block for a start-up. Money is always tight for start-ups, and an otherwise perfect candidate might have salary expectations that are out of line with your budget. If this is the case, do not underestimate the value a good office manager brings to the clinic; they are the backbone of your practice and will more than pay for themselves.

When you find the right person be sure to prepare an employment agreement. It should include, but not be limited to:

- Job title and responsibilities

- Compensation package

- Work hours and schedule

- Vacation time

- Sick time and pay

- Restrictive covenants (i.e., Non-solicitation, confidentiality, and non-disclosure)

- Termination details (including severance pay, if applicable)

When to Hire Your First Hygienist

Many start-up dentists postpone hiring a dental hygienist until their practice gets busier. As a start-up, you will likely have gaps in your appointment calendar, so it makes sense to spend some time with patients looking after their hygiene. What better way to create a long-term relationship with your patient?

The Interview Process

Even if you have hired a professional office manager, my advice is to keep control of the interview process yourself. By all means involve the office manager, but do not delegate interviewing to them. Hiring decisions are your responsibility.

There are many methods of interviewing job candidates, and I urge you to do a little research and find one that feels comfortable and fits the hiring of dental staff. Here are a few general tips to get you started.

1. Avoid the common "ping-pong" interviewing technique, where you ask a question, the candidate answers it, and you ask another question. The challenge with this approach is that you listen less as you formulate or anticipate the next question you will ask. Actively listening to the candidate's answers and watching their body language is a crucial part of the interview process. Try asking all your questions upfront (obviously, not too many) and then sit back and let the applicant do all the talking.

2. Telling the candidate too much about yourself can result in savvy applicants keying into your personality and telling you precisely what you want to hear. Instead, use open-ended questions such as:

    a. What would your former colleagues and your former employer say about you?

    b. What are the things you liked about the last practice you worked at, and what did you dislike?

    c. What changes would you have made there if you'd had the opportunity?

    d. What accomplishments are you most proud of?

    e. What do you enjoy doing in your spare time?

    f. What is the last book you read?

    Listen actively and carefully to the answers, and where appropriate, probe further with follow-up questions. Remember, résumés are usually boilerplate; you need to discover the person hiding behind the résumé.

3. Make the candidate feel at ease. You gain nothing by making an interview more stressful than it already is for the applicant. Offering them water, tea, or coffee can make them more relaxed. It also allows you to see how they interact with the person who brings the beverage. Did they acknowledge them and say thank you? Did they offer to clear away the glass or mug at the end of the interview? Did they push their chair back under the table or desk? Small things, maybe, but they tell you a lot about people.

4. If you feel a candidate deserves a second interview, consider inviting the person to come to the office for one day to observe and work with you. Ensure your staff has plenty of opportunities to talk and interact with the person.

5. Always check the references. Talking to someone's references can be eye-opening. Sure, no one gives a person as a reference who they believe will speak about them detrimentally, but with a bit of digging and a lot of listening, you may learn whether the person would hire them again, and if not, why not?

Introducing New Staff

You will have an organizational culture in mind for your practice. It will consist of all the things you liked about the places you have worked and all the things you wished were different. Your new practice will reflect you as a person, your morals, ethics, the atmosphere you want the clinic to have, team spirit and camaraderie, the level of customer service, the patient experience, and more.

There is no better time for you to share your vision for the practice than when someone first becomes a member of your team. You must prepare and mold them to fit the organizational culture you desire. Many dentists do a poor job of orienting new staff members. If you want a dedicated and highly skilled employee, you must invest time and energy to nurture them toward professional success.

Here are some things to consider:

1. Provide job descriptions for every staff member. A job description

provides clear direction and outlines expectations.

2. Take training seriously and create a training schedule for new employees. Be active in your employees' training—it's your practice, and getting it right from the start is crucial. Cross-train wherever possible so the clinic continues running smoothly when a key employee calls in sick or is on vacation.

3. Give a trusted employee a mentorship role over a new employee. Peer mentorship will help ensure a smooth transition of the new staff member into the practice. The mentor's role is to familiarize the new person with the unwritten policies and culture of the practice and generally show them the ropes. A mentor provides a new employee with an example of the behavior required to be successful in their new environment.

Creating a Championship Team

The success of your new practice depends on the quality of your team, much in the same way that a hockey team won't reach the Stanley Cup playoffs without working together and playing off each other's strengths. What strategies do you need to employ to create your championship team?

1. Understand that your job is not to control people; your mission is to build a team.

2. Start by assuming everybody on your team wants to do a fantastic job every day.

3. Recruit the most skilled player you can find for each position. Remember, however, that a positive attitude is the number one trait you are looking for in an employee.

4. Look for employees who understand and embrace the essential truth that when it comes to teams, the sum is greater than the individual parts and that success as a team is more important than personal ambitions.

5. Establish what success looks like and the level of performance you expect from each team member.

6. Compensate employees based on their performance. Not all hockey players on a team receive equal remuneration.

7. Never be afraid to replace people who consistently underperform.

8. Be a constant source of enthusiasm and inspiration to your team. Lead from the front.

9. Acknowledge team members at every opportunity. There is no greater need for an individual in the workplace than to be appreciated.

10. When a team member falters, support them; use your coaching and management skills to help them avoid the same error in the future, and then move on, don't dwell on their mistake.

11. Be there for your team. Have an open-door policy.

12. Practice objective, not subjective, decision-making.

13. Create a safe and supportive environment and allow team members to share freely, knowing that you will keep what they say in the strictest confidence.

14. Be authentic and take full responsibility.

15. Celebrate success freely, and applaud each team member's growth.

16. Embrace change.

It may be a bold statement, but your employees are more critical than your patients to your success, so treat them well. Treat them as you would your best patient; remember, you need them more than they need you. Would you prefer your favorite patient or your hygienist to move to another dentist? The financial impact of a patient leaving your practice is minimal compared to the economic upheaval that results from downtime in your hygiene department.

> **Purtzki's Law:** Employees are more critical than patients to your success. Remember you need them more than they need you.

Having watched countless associates take their first faltering steps into practice ownership, I can categorically say that at this moment in time there have never been so many opportunities to build a successful practice. That is, if you have a fantastic team behind you. By getting the HR side of your practice running smoothly, you will avoid the constant worry your dental colleagues have about keeping their clinic fully staffed with enthusiastic and committed staff. More importantly, when your associate leaves to set up her own clinic down the line, you won't be concerned with their ability to poach your staff.

9

Managing for Success

"No one can whistle a symphony; it takes an orchestra to play it."
— Halford Luccock

I love going to the symphony. Recently, while listening to Beethoven's Eroica Symphony, I watched as the conductor helped the orchestra convey the piece's drama and sense of urgency. On the drive home later, it struck me there are similarities between an orchestra conductor and a dentist. I know that may seem like a stretch, but bear with me. A conductor and a dentist must manage a group of people playing specialist roles; more importantly, they must work as a cohesive team. Beyond that, they have to meet or exceed their patron's expectations because their financial success is directly linked to the number of people they can attract to see them "play."

Our two leaders must hire the best people for each position and work within budgetary constraints. They have to translate their vision to their team, which takes time (rehearsals for the conductor, staff training for the dentist).

Audiences regularly reward the players in an orchestra with applause. In a dental clinic, employees may receive individual thanks from patients, but "applause" needs to come from you. Morning huddles, staff meetings, and one-on-one mentoring can be ways to reenergize your employees. Be assured that you can never overdo acknowledging your team for who they are and what they are accomplishing.

Let's look at how you set yourself up for success. First, identify your core objectives, for example:

- High levels of patient satisfaction
- Satisfied and motivated team members
- Optimal financial performance

Patient Satisfaction

Inside my desk drawer, I taped a quotation by Zig Ziglar, the legendary sales trainer. I read it every time I open the drawer; it helps keep my focus on customer service. It reads, "You can have anything in life that you want if you just give enough people what they want."

If you prioritize the needs of your patients, they will reciprocate by being loyal to your practice. They will show appreciation, pay promptly, accept your suggested treatment plans, and recommend you to their family and friends. Your management focus should always be on your patients if you want a successful practice. This simple yet powerful concept will help you to build your practice quickly. Instill in your team that it is not you who pay their salaries but satisfied patients.

Building a successful practice from scratch means exceeding every patient's expectations. You do this by understanding that it doesn't matter how good you think your service has been, but how much the patients value it.

Consider this formula:

Perceived Value = Perception – Expectation

A *satisfied* patient feels that the service *met* their expectations. This patient has little to no investment in your clinic. If convenient, they may or may not revisit your clinic. These patients don't help you build your practice because they are unlikely to recommend you to others.

Loyal patients are people who perceive that your value of service *exceeded* their expectations. You have provided an exceptional, positive experience. To create loyal patients and turn them into raving fans, you must provide them with a memorable experience, not just once but every time they visit the clinic. The question is, how can you turn a routine dental visit into a great experience?

1. Your clinic must exude an air of positive energy. You and your team must be enthusiastic. This high-performance atmosphere only occurs when everyone is happy at work and loves what they are doing. One of the best definitions of selling I have heard is simply "the transfer of enthusiasm." For example, if you feel passionate about your proposed dental treatment plan for a patient, the patient will be more likely to accept the treatment without little to no objection.

2. Successful dentists love what they do, and it shows. They and their staff are fired up and excited about their work.

3. Beyond attitude, positive first impressions are also crucial. How you look and sound is as important as your enthusiasm. Imagine an enthusiastic, likable dentist who unfortunately has long, unkempt hair, and is wearing dirty, torn (not in a fashionable way) jeans. The lack of professionalism would make most patients think twice about their dentistry skills and hygiene protocols.

4. Second and third impressions also play their part in ensuring patients will return and support recommended treatment plans. If you talk down to patients or drown them in technical jargon, they will glaze over. Match your vocabulary to that of the patient, and they will feel more at ease.

5. Provide a minimal-stress environment—many patients are nervous. You can't stop patients from hearing high-speed drills, but you can help them relax by making the waiting room calm, peaceful, and comfortable. Staff can be welcoming and attentive. When they see you share stories, ask about their family, and tell a joke (be careful that your humor is politically correct—I find kids' jokes safe territory), they will feel comfortable and at ease.

Once you have morphed your *satisfied* customers into *loyal* fans, keep them that way—don't take your foot off the gas. Show your appreciation by arranging special appointment times, calling them in the evening to see how they feel after a non-routine treatment, or sending them the occasional card or small gift. Don't overdo it; small gestures mean a lot to people, especially when your competitors are less than accommodating. I know one dentist who gave a longstanding patient a 25th-anniversary cake. That patient posted about the gift extensively on social media, and the dentist has indicated he will take him for lunch on their upcoming 30th anniversary.

Let's revisit the formula: ***Perceived Value = Perception − Expectation.*** If a patient's perceived value is unrealistic, it will be difficult for you to exceed expectations. The trick is to manage perceived value and keep patients' expectations realistic. The key is to under-promise and over-deliver

Patient relationships should never be left to chance. Your ability to provide consistent, quality service to your patients is critical to your practice's success. To accomplish this, you must have a top-notch, patient-driven service system. But how do you build such a system?

Moments of Truth

Consider Jan Carlzon's "Moments of Truth" model from his book of the same name. It will help you and your staff stay focused on providing top-quality service. It is an excellent tool that can help you manage patient relationships. Karl Albrecht expanded on the concept in his book *Service America.*

A moment-of-truth is "An episode in which a patient comes into contact with some aspect of your practice and forms an impression of the quality of service." Providing excellent service requires all your patients' moments of truth are positive. The trick is to constantly manage these moments of truth to prevent service quality from drifting into mediocrity.

Patient contact occurs multiple times during a *cycle of service;* a series of events in which you and your staff try to meet patient expectations at each point. Typically, the cycle begins at the first contact point with a patient when they call for an appointment or walk in off the street.

First, identify the particular cycles of service in your practice. You may have different service cycles for hygiene, emergency, routine, or big-case patients. In each cycle, identify the various moments of truth. Next, take each moment of truth and segregate it into what Karl Albrecht identifies as three components:

1. *The Standard Expectation:* the minimal expectation your patient has for any given moment of truth.

2. *Experience Detractors:* an occasion where the patient experiences a specific moment of truth, and the experience is negative.

3. *Experience Enhancers:* a situation where the patient comes into contact with a moment of truth and the experience is exceptional—beyond expectations.

A cycle of service example from the patient's perspective might be:

    a. I called the office for an appointment because I had a toothache.

    b. I went to the office and waited for treatment.

    c. I received treatment.

    d. I settled my account.

    e. I left the office.

    f. The pain is fading.

The example above involves six moments of truth. Let's dissect the first moment of truth. "I called the office for an appointment because I had a toothache."

Standard Expectations

1. Someone answered the phone on the third ring.

2. The receptionist seemed competent and helpful.

3. I received my appointment within a reasonable time.

Experience Detractors

1. The phone was unanswered after three rings.

2. The telephone answering message asked me to leave my phone number.

3. They put me on hold for what seemed like an eternity.

4. I could hardly understand what the receptionist was saying.

5. I had to wait an unreasonably long time for my appointment.

Experience Enhancer

1. The phone was answered on the first ring.

2. The receptionist answered in a cheerful voice, gave her name, and asked how she could help me. I felt immediately at ease.

3. The receptionist recognized my voice before I had a chance to introduce myself.

4. The receptionist showed great empathy and a sense of urgency in finding me an immediate solution for my pain.

5. The receptionist arranged for a same-day appointment.

Cash Flow Up, Stress Down? Thank Pareto!

In 1906 the Italian economist Pareto astutely observed that twenty percent of the population owned eighty percent of the country's wealth. This is commonly referred to as the 80/20 rule. How does that theory apply to the success of your practice?

- The small percentage of high-maintenance, low-revenue patients cause the vast majority of hassle. These patients are never satisfied and will suck the energy out of you and your staff.

- Twenty percent of dental procedures account for eighty percent of revenue. If you have sufficient practice volume, consider adding an associate to handle the less profitable work.

- Pamper your highest revenue-generating, most loyal patients with small gifts, lots of extra attention, preferred appointments, etc.

- Delegate. Before you start any task, ask yourself whether it is taking you away from more profitable work. If so, ask another staff member to handle the job.

- The 80/20 principle works when it comes to staff too. Twenty percent of employees are producing eighty percent of the profit-making results. Nurture those stars and make those who are good, excellent.

Happy and Motivated Team Members

Management success relies on creating a team that works well together as a cohesive unit. You are responsible for communicating effectively and involving the team in practice decisions concerning all employees. In my experience, the dentists who maintain a positive and enthusiastic attitude and regularly acknowledge team members for doing a good job are far more successful.

One way to ensure a unified team is to provide every staff member with a job description. Here are two simple examples.

Office Manager

The responsibility of the office manager is to plan, direct and control all aspects of the practice's operation. The scope of responsibility includes increasing profitability through patient service, team development, and financial management. Duties include, but are not limited to:

- Assisting the dentist with hiring, firing, and retention

- Maintaining employee relations

- Ensuring the health and safety of staff and patients

- Performance management through training and development

  - Coach team members to exceed patient expectations. For example, teach staff how to interact with patients and build their trust by asking about their hobbies, what they do for a living, their children or grandchildren, and, especially these days, discovering the personal pronouns they prefer. Patient trust increases when they feel heard and understood, and conversations become more relevant.

- Customer service—In particular, handling unsatisfied patients and taking remedial action where necessary

- Monitoring financial projections and preparing weekly and monthly financial summaries to help the practice achieve its targets

- Optimizing patient appointment schedules through good treatment plan management and patient contact

- Facilitating team meetings to improve the quality of patient interaction and enhance team productivity

Dental Assistant

As a clinical support team member, the dental assistant ensures that the clinical department provides patients with the highest quality dental care in a safe environment. Duties include:

- Maintaining clinical supplies inventory

- Supervising maintenance of clinical equipment

- Ensuring a clean and sanitized operatory

- Escorting patients to the treatment room

- Completing patient charts
- Updating each patient's health history
- Ensuring every patient enjoys a positive experience
- Personal career development through continuing education

Optimizing Financial Performance

High-performing dental practices have tight control of their management accounts. Their office managers are on top of income statements and monitor income with an eye on the clinic's projections. A good office manager will quickly know when remedial action is necessary, ensuring the practice's revenues don't fall behind. Supervising financial performance allows an office manager to alert the dentist about areas that require attention. These include:

Total Revenue Versus Budget

The monthly budgets you prepared to get bank financing will come in handy to measure how your actual results compare to your projections.

Staff Costs as a Percentage of Revenue

Since staff costs are semi-fixed, they do not fluctuate with revenues. Until you need additional staff, monitor how staff costs decline as a percentage of revenues. You can also project what effect hiring another team member will have on the clinic's bottom line.

Number of New Patients Per Month

Ensure you count the number of actual new patients to the clinic. By "actual," I mean exclude patients who followed you from your previous employer. One dentist I worked with was thrilled when fifty to sixty new patients per month arrived at his clinic right after opening. This number was higher than he had predicted, so he decided to delay the implementation of his marketing plan.

Unfortunately, after four months, the "new" patient flow slowed to only ten new patients per month. I pointed out that most of his "new" patients initially came from his previous clinic. He implemented his marketing plan, but the delay meant it took some time to reach his target of fifty new patients per month.

Dental Supplies as a Percentage of Revenue

Purtzki's Law: Dental supplies account for approximately ten percent of revenues in existing dental practices. However, in start-up dental practices they account for around five percent.

Dental supplies account for approximately ten percent of revenues in existing dental practices. However, in start-up dental practices they account for around five percent. Why is this? In start-ups, the dentist orders supplies and, because they have to watch expenditures carefully, they search for better prices. Once a staff member begins to handle the buying, no matter how diligent they may be, they focus less on price. When it's your money, you are a heck of a lot more careful. If you are not ordering supplies, I advise limiting your buyer's budget to five percent of gross revenues.

Conversion of Patient Calls to Patient Visits

No matter how sophisticated your marketing system is, how well-designed and interactive your website is, and how active you are on social media, success ultimately comes down to how many prospective patients you close. If your receptionist is well-trained, it should not be difficult for them to book appointments for nine out of ten first-time callers. Be mindful that new patients are any clinic's lifeblood, even more so for a start-up.

Key Performance Indicators (KPIs)

Key performance indicators (KPIs) are indispensable for managing a dental practice. KPIs measure past performance and highlight opportunities to grow your practice. For instance, a KPI that determines the amount of revenue generated by various marketing sources, e.g., postcards, social media, newsletters, word of mouth, and walk-ins, among others, is invaluable if you want to ensure higher returns on your marketing dollars.

Another KPI might track wait times for hygiene patients and help assess whether it makes economic sense to reduce wait times by hiring an additional hygienist to meet demand.

With increasing competition in the dental industry, KPIs are invaluable to ensure you grow your practice profitably.

10

The First Thirty Days

From the day you open your clinic, the clock is counting down on your first thirty days of operation, and you have a lot to do if you are going to make it a success. Think of it like this: on day one you have a 50/50 chance of success, but everything you do from day one will either increase or reduce that probability.

The first month of a clinic's life presents many challenges, but the biggest is how you allocate your time. Your new clinic won't have a full slate of patients waiting for you on day one, so should you continue to work as an associate for a few days a week until patient volume justifies your gradual transfer to the new clinic full-time? The pro side of this strategy is that you can maximize your earnings to inject much-needed working capital into the clinic for the first six months, and provide for your living expenses. The negative to this strategy is how much it costs your new practice when you are only a part-time dentist.

Let's be a fly on the wall of your new clinic a week before the grand opening. You are standing at the clinic's front window, looking at a busy thoroughfare. You are metaphorically patting yourself on the back and thinking, "Yes, I was right to pay a premium for this lease space; look at all the cars and pedestrians passing by."

Scenario One

Consider how your first thirty days might look with you at the helm full-time in this first scenario. In the scene above, many of those people passing by notice your new clinic. They are curious to check out the facility—and, of course, you. If they like what they see; that is, a friendly professional-looking dentist, a clean, hi-tech, friendly, and warm ambiance, and plenty of open appointments to choose from, it's likely that they will sign up as a new patient. In this scenario you have created a golden opportunity to cultivate close relationships built on trust. Excitement about the new dentist on the block spills over to their friends and family, who also check you out.

Once they have received treatment and experienced outstanding customer service, they will again talk about their experience to friends, family, and on social media. Your clinic lived up to its hype. New patients, as opposed to existing patients, are far more likely to rave about you and give you the most referrals. They are vital to your long-term success.

Scenario Two

How will your first thirty days pan out if you decide to remain an associate at another clinic for several days a week?

As in scenario one, potential new patients walk through the door to see what the new clinic is all about and are greeted by your front desk person. The place is quiet because you are working at another clinic. There is a subdued ambiance. Despite the lack of activity and the fact they don't have an opportunity to meet you, the clinic looks new, fresh, clean, and modern, so some walk-ins try to make an appointment. Unfortunately, appointment times are limited because you only work a few days a week at the clinic. They can't get their preferred day or time but book a less convenient time anyway. They leave, wondering whether they made the right choice. Others say they will return when they can meet the dentist (they don't); it is the equivalent of "just looking." Unfortunately, you never get a second chance to make a first impression.

> **Purtzki's Law:** The fewer hours you work in your clinic, the lower your new patient count. You are your clinic's oxygen; without you breathing life into it, it will fail to thrive.

To Be, Or Not To Be, an Associate

After reading the two scenarios above, I wouldn't blame you for thinking that you need to ditch the associate job and be at your new clinic 24/7, but hold on, it's not all or nothing; you just need to get the balance correct. I suggest you remain an associate, maybe working two to three days a week, but aim to be at your new clinic for at least four days a week. And, choose those days and times wisely—that is, during busier periods.

Hopefully, if you followed my advice earlier in this book you asked for and received a generous line of credit, one which provides financial support to cover the start-up phase until the clinic breaks even and revenues cover all practice expenses.

As I mentioned above, you can easily calculate your associate income and the amount available to support the clinic. Still, it is far harder to estimate the cost of only working in your new clinic part-time as it affects new-patient growth.

It is worthwhile spending some time playing with the numbers. Here is an example to get you started:

Assumption 1: You work four days in your clinic and add fifty new patients monthly per your initial cash flow projections. The annual financial projections are:

Gross Revenues $500,000
Expenses $250,000
Net Income $250,000

Assumption 2: Your original projection was fifty new patients per month, but you decided to work only two days a week in your clinic. This results in a growth of only thirty patients per month. The annual financial projections are:

Gross Revenues $300,000
Expenses $220,000
Net Income $80,000

As you can see, working fewer days resulted in a $170,000 reduction in net income. This significant drop is due to most of your practice expenses, such as salaries, rent, etc., being fixed. Other costs are variable and relate directly to dental work carried out (i.e., dental supplies, lab fees, etc.). The question is, can you earn $170,000 in associate income to cover this loss? Unlikely. Even if that were possible, the bigger picture challenge is the lack of growth in your new clinic and its effect on future revenue.

Only you can decide the correct balance between working as an associate and working in your new clinic. However, consider the time spent in your clinic as time spent growing your future. An analogy is buying a house instead of renting; when you pay a mortgage, you are investing in your future and paying the mortgage down while the value of your home, over time, increases. When you rent, the amount you pay goes to the landlord, which helps them pay their mortgage down while they sit back and watch the value of their property grow. Do you want to invest in your future or that of the dentist for whom you work?

Start-Up Marketing Strategies

Practice Website

A good practice website is essential. Those people driving or walking past your door may check you out online. For patients, online booking is a big selling point. Add informative content in the form of a blog, with information directly relevant to your existing patients and those looking for a new dentist. All blogs and articles should be search engine optimized—that is, they need to contain SEO-rich content.

Google Reviews

On your website, have a direct link to Google so patients can easily leave a review. You can also send this link to patients when you send them reminders or statements.

Social Media Platforms

Before opening the doors to your clinic for the first time, you must ensure you have a solid social media presence. This should include a website and the social media platforms your patients are most likely to use. Don't try to be on every platform; choose the ones that make sense for your practice. Consider Facebook to reach a general audience, encourage patient conversation, build loyalty, and attract new patients. Instagram is popular, especially with millennials, but you will need interesting visual content. LinkedIn is good for reaching a slightly more mature market of professionals. In all cases, you will need to designate a person responsible for keeping your social media presence up to date with new and exciting content.

Having an online presence and being active on social media is not enough to ensure success; you will need a diverse marketing strategy to keep those inquiries and walk-ins coming through the door.

Email Marketing

Collect email addresses from your patients as a matter of course, and use them to promote new products or services, offer discounts, promote procedures such as tooth whitening, and provide tips on oral hygiene. The method of regular engagement with patients helps to build the clinic's relationship with patients and also builds loyalty.

Direct Mail

Direct mail is becoming increasingly common after almost fading away when email campaigns became so prevalent. Today, direct mail is an excellent way to introduce you, your staff, and your new clinic to people specifically interested in, and in need of, your services.

Simple postcards are back! In my experience, delivering postcards to neighborhood residences can generate many new patient leads. You must send them out multiple times to achieve the full benefit and get the best results. Promote what makes you different (e.g., extended hours, weekend appointments, free coffee, free parking, the latest technology, a therapy dog for nervous patients, specials such as a free exam, discounted teeth whitening, or a free consultation).

You are a professional, so get a professional designer to create your postcard and get it printed by a print company. Don't use your office inkjet! Here's an inside tip: women choose the family dentist, so design accordingly. And, don't forget to add your phone number and web address big and bold; you want people to call the clinic to make an appointment or check out your website for more information.

Newspaper Advertisements

Local community newspapers give you the best bang for your buck. Not only that, they will often feature your new clinic in an article.

Case Study

A short time ago, I worked with a client to drive more traffic to her clinic by promoting a $99 Zoom teeth whitening special. The goal was to bring in new, long-term patients. Before launching the campaign, I researched what prices other dental offices were charging for teeth whitening to ensure we were competitive.

We advertised in the local newspaper, mailed out postcards, and promoted the offer on the clinic website. In addition, we dropped business cards and promotional postcards to spas, nail clinics, beauticians, aestheticians, and hair salons throughout the neighborhood.

We carefully tracked every element of the campaign. The newspaper advertisement attracted the largest number of people due to its broad circulation, but all methods brought people to the clinic. What clinic staff found interesting was that almost everyone who came for teeth whitening stated they had come for the special only and had no interest in switching dentists. My client was astounded when eighty percent of the people who took advantage of the Zoom special, subsequently became patients. Why? Again, we followed up with each patient, and it was the design and ambiance of the clinic itself and the warm welcome by the staff and the dentist.

Grand Opening

Once your marketing strategy has had a chance to make an impact and your online presence is creating a buzz, you should introduce your clinic to the community. A grand opening is a marvelous way to meet people in a social setting rather than against a backdrop of dental drills or from behind a reception desk. However, timing is everything. It's tempting to have the grand opening a few days before you start seeing patients, but I advise waiting a couple of weeks. Let the paint dry, give the contractor time to fix the deficiencies, and allow your staff time to get used to how the clinic operates. This lag time will also allow you to promote the event widely to ensure an impressive turnout.

I suggest you hold your grand opening on a weekend when families have time to attend. Make it a family affair with entertainment, food, and games that parents and children can appreciate. If possible, invite a local celebrity to hang out with the families and sign autographs; sports stars are particularly popular. Invite the local radio station to be part of the festivities; this is easier if you advertise with them. If you are advertising on local radio, they may attend, and broadcast from, your event. This can offer exceptional coverage.

Inviting a large number of people at one time can cause parking headaches, so consider offering valet parking. Perhaps a local charity could supply the valets in return for a donation. If you decide to do this, ensure you have adequate insurance.

In my experience, if handled well, grand openings can result in a considerable number of new patients signing up.

Ongoing Community Involvement

Committing to your community as a long-term investment will pay dividends. Make it your goal to meet with the managers and coaches of your local sports teams. Discuss how you might financially support the team and families who might be struggling to pay for equipment and membership fees.

I remember one client who got a considerable boost in new patients when he offered free, fitted mouthguards to children. His clinic was not yet running at full capacity, so his staff had time to handle the workload. Local parents were thrilled that their children no longer had to use uncomfortable, ill-fitting mouthguards from local sports equipment retailers. When people get something for free, they feel a desire to reciprocate, but still, it was amazing the number of families who became clinic patients. And as you know, young families make the best patients because you will have them for a long time. In addition, this dentist made donations to local sports clubs specifically to reduce membership fees.

Know What Marketing Dollars Are Working

In those early days, you invest a lot of money in marketing. Very soon the question becomes, which marketing methods are giving me a return on my investment, and which are like throwing my hard-earned money away?

Create a checklist with all the ways people might have heard about your clinic. When someone calls your receptionist or walks through the door, they simply need to ask, "That's wonderful. May I ask how you heard about us?" They then annotate the checklist. The list should include not only advertising sources but also things like word-of-mouth, they walked past the door and saw your sign, their friend is a patient, etc.

Sales

It seems strange to talk about sales in terms of a dental clinic; most dentists don't like to think of themselves as being in business, but at the end of the day you need new patients to survive. The ability of your receptionist to convert a phone inquiry into an appointment or a clinic visit is crucial to your success. The same is true of walk-ins; they should immediately be converted to appointments. It is a critically important job.

Patient attraction is ultimately your responsibility. I recommend that my clients check their phone logs daily and follow up on calls from those prospective patients who did not make an appointment. If you are not achieving a reasonable closing rate, consider hiring a specialist consultant who works for dental practices to teach staff to convert phone calls to appointments.

Cash Management

Cash flow can be scary in those first thirty days. Deposits are few; bills are many. Ensure your office manager has an accounting system that allows you to monitor your cash flow weekly. Schedule a weekly meeting with your office manager to review the clinic's bank balance, available line of credit, unpaid invoices, and payment due dates for invoices before they accrue interest.

The bank set up the line of credit to provide adequate start-up funding. If you run into unforeseen expenses and are concerned the credit line will not be sufficient, don't wait—talk to your bank manager immediately. Keeping a close eye on your cash flow will mitigate the chances of your bank bouncing your cheques. If that happens, it will negatively affect your credit rating, and the bank could call in the loan if it gets out of hand.

Customer (or Rather, Patient) Service

When a new patient walks into your clinic, their first impression will be of the interior, the décor, the ambiance, the temperature, the smell, and the sounds. It will immediately assault their senses for good or bad. Seconds later, hopefully, a staff member will greet them, which will be their second impression. At that point, you are either exceeding their expectations or disappointing them. They are either more inclined to make an appointment or less.

In those first few seconds, you have an opportunity to secure a new patient—possibly for several decades. You have now entered the realm of customer service. Excel and your patient numbers rise, disappoint, and your patient numbers go down.

In my experience, the approach taken by the Ritz-Carlton chain of hotels offers an excellent blueprint for wowing patients. Its customer service culture is legendary and starts with the maxim, "We Are Ladies and Gentlemen Serving Ladies and Gentlemen!" The implication is that employees must treat workplace colleagues with the same dignity as guests.

How does the company deliver on this promise? The basics are simple; instruct employees always to offer guests a warm and sincere greeting using their name if possible. They must anticipate the guest's needs and comply with their requests. Finally, employees must address guests by name, say goodbye, and wish them well when they leave.

Employees use affirmative words in all communication with guests, such as "no problem," "absolutely," and "my pleasure." Employees are empowered to solve problems immediately without checking with a supervisor, and they have access to a set amount of funds to resolve issues instantly. Consider how this might work in your clinic; you might allow your receptionist discretionary power to lower a patient's bill if they complain about waiting an inordinately long time to see the dentist. This revolutionary idea could increase customer loyalty.

To implement Ritz-Carlton's "culture of service," you must have frequent employee huddles focusing exclusively on customer service. Combining first-class customer service with first-class clinical care will boost new patient referrals and case acceptance. If customer service and convenience become your top priorities, you will attract loyal patients to your practice.

Patients should feel a sense of belonging. They should feel they are special and treated with respect. They should be special. When they finish their treatment and pay their bill, even when it is a significant sum, they should feel it was worth it—that they got value for money.

What values do you want to inspire in your staff? What are your expectations for appropriate behavior, team spirit, and the practices and protocols which will be the glue that holds the practice together?

During the first thirty days, you will create your clinic's culture. Get it right, and you will be a patient magnet and attract the best staff. Don't underestimate your first month; it is the foundation on which you will build the next thirty years.

A

Acknowledgements

First, I'd like to thank Mike Wicks, my collaborator on this book. He helped me find my voice and made the book both readable and accessible. His commitment and passion for the book were motivating. He helped make the whole process enjoyable and a lot easier than I ever thought possible.

Thank you to the Blue Beetle Books publishing team. Paul Abra for handling production and promotion, Tom Spetter for designing such an amazing jacket and for laying the book out with such style, Kara Anderson for her considerable copyediting skills, Sheila Wicks for proofreading the final manuscript to ensure there were no embarrassing typos, and finally Mike Wicks for his ongoing publishing guidance.

Finally, I want to thank my wife Marie for her encouragement and unconditional support. Without her, I would never have been able to write this book.

Praise for Manfred Purtzki's Books

"Navigating the biggest decision of your life without the benefit of 35 years of experience is precisely what you're doing ... why not mitigate that risk by reading Manfred Purtzki's book ... best money you'll ever spend."

~ Dr. Kevin Lathangue, B.Sc., D.M.D

"This step-by-step guide to ensuring a successful purchase and transition is a must read for any dentist considering buying a dental practice."

~ Dr. Ken Horng

"Purtzki's book offers a comprehensive and practical guide to buying a dental practice. His advice on how to negotiate successfully with sellers is especially valuable."

~ Dr. Polly Chan

"Thank you for assembling all of the information required for a successful sale in one well written, easy to read document. This should be the go-to document for every dentist."

~ Dr. Ron Smith (CDA, Past president)

"The book is full of great tips and pearls of wisdom, great to read before you sell a practice or even buy one."

~ Dr. Jehan Casey

"I wish I had read this coming out of dental school, it would have totally changed the arc of my trajectory once I settled in and began my practice. Frankly, it never occurred to me back then that I could even sell my practice. Manfred Purtzki truly understands buying and selling dental practices—he has a deep empathy with dentists. This book helps you build a dental practice that offers premium service, thus increasing its value and ultimate selling price. It is an absolutely essential read for all dentists regardless of age or practice status."

~ Dr. Dean Nomura

Notes:

9 781777 828745